M24 Chaffee

by David Doyle

Walk Around®

Covers and art by Don Greer
Illustrations by Matheu Spraggins

When American-built armor first went up against Axis forces, notably in North Africa, it quickly became apparent that the 37mm cannon mounted on many of the U.S. vehicles was simply inadequate against the tough armor of their adversaries. The relatively tall silhouette inherent from using radial engines was also a deficiency, as was the slab-sided construction of many of these vehicles.

The M24 was developed in order to address all of these concerns, and more. Armed with a 75mm main gun, the Chaffee, as the M24 was dubbed, was able to dispatch many of the foes that had daunted its 37mm predecessors. Designated M5, the cannon was based on the T13E1 developed for the nose of the B25H bomber. Guns originally intended for use on bombers are identifiable by the grooved collar near the muzzle that had engaged the concentric recoil mechanism of the AN-M9 aircraft mount. This collar is not present on later-production guns manufactured expressly for tanks.

The power plant of the M24 was taken over from the M5A1, and consisted of twin Cadillac engines and Hydramatic transmissions. The M5A1's automatic transfer case was not highly regarded and was replaced in the M24 with a two-speed manual transfer box.

Both the driver and assistant driver were provided with operator's controls, and the assistant driver was provided with a .30-caliber machine gun in a ball mount.

The M24 was equipped with torsion bar suspension, which gave the vehicle a lower profile and smoother ride than earlier light tanks had had. The suspension also made the M24 a more stable firing platform.

Production of the new vehicle began before it had been type classified as standard, with both Cadillac and Massey-Harris receiving contracts to produce the new T24 light tank. Cadillac was awarded its contract in April 1944 and Massey-Harris received its contract in July that year. Also in July the new tank was classified as standard and designated M24. By war's end 4,731 Chaffees had been produced.

Late-production tanks had mounting pads for flotation equipment on the hull. A postwar rebuilding program processed 1,600 tanks before it came to an end in 1950. As the M24 was replaced by the M41 in US service, the surplus Chaffees were supplied to friendly nations, and continued to be fielded well into the 1970s.

Acknowledgments

All photos were taken by the author unless otherwise credited.

The vehicles shown in this book are owned by the Veterans Memorial Museum, Huntsville, Alabama; the Ropkey Armor Museum; the National Museum of Americans in Wartime; Brent Mullins; Joe Garbarino; and the Patton Museum.

This book would not have been possible without the generous assistance of Tom Kailbourn; Randy Withrow and his staff in Huntsville; Fred and Lani Ropkey and Skip Warvel at the Ropkey Armor Museum in Crawfordsville, Indiana; Joe Garbarino; Allan Cors and Marc Sehring at The National Museum of Americans in Wartime; David E. Harper; Chris Hughes; Brent Mullins; Scott Taylor; and especially Denise Moss – who patiently traveled with me coast to coast hauling the gear to take these photos.

About the Walk Around®/On Deck Series®

The Walk Around®/On Deck® series is about the details of specific military equipment using color and black-and-white archival photographs and photographs of in-service, preserved, and restored equipment. *Walk Around®* titles are devoted to aircraft and military vehicles, while *On Deck®* titles are devoted to warships. They are picture books of 80 pages, focusing on operational equipment, not one-off or experimental subjects.

Copyright 2009 Squadron/Signal Publications
1115 Crowley Drive, Carrollton, TX 75006-1312 U.S.A.
Printed in the U.S.A.

ISBN 978-0-89747-592-1

Military/Combat Photographs and Snapshots

If you have any photos of aircraft, armor, soldiers, or ships of any nation, particularly wartime snapshots, please share them with us and help make Squadron/Signal's books all the more interesting and complete in the future. Any photograph sent to us will be copied and returned. Electronic images are preferred. The donor will be fully credited for any photos used. Please send them to:

Squadron/Signal Publications
1115 Crowley Drive
Carrollton, TX 75006-1312 U.S.A.
www.SquadronSignalPublications.com

(Title Page) A restored M24 in the collection of The National Museum of Americans in Wartime displays the still-modern appearance of the Chaffee, designed in 1943.

(Front Cover) The 740th Tank Battalion, attached to the 82nd Airborne Division, operated in Belgium during the winter of 1944-45. This tank exhibits the unit's typical winter camouflage of overall white.

(Back Cover) The M24 Chaffee rolled into battle again during the Korean War. These tankers guard an intersection during the summer of 1950, their tank already showing the signs of the then-only weeks-old war.

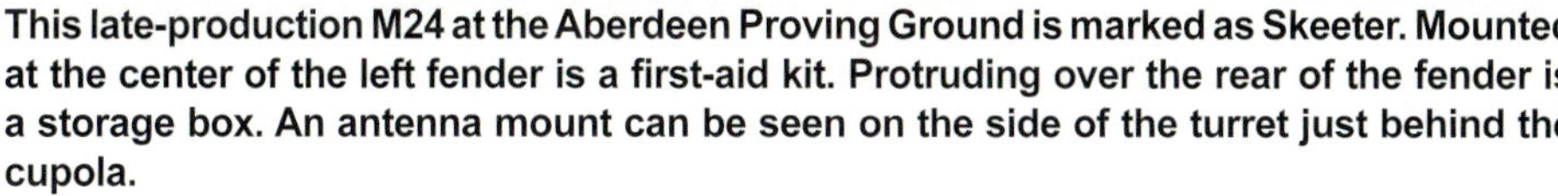

This late-production M24 at the Aberdeen Proving Ground is marked as Skeeter. Mounted at the center of the left fender is a first-aid kit. Protruding over the rear of the fender is a storage box. An antenna mount can be seen on the side of the turret just behind the cupola.

This side view of M24 Skeeter shows to good effect the small, curved piece of armor plate that extended from the right side of the turret. It was designed to protect the .50-caliber antiaircraft machine gun from frontal fire when stored on the side of the turret, to the rear of the plate.

In this frontal view of a late-production M24 at Aberdeen, mounting plates for the flotation device are visible on the front of the final-drive housings, as are the mounting bracket for the detachable driver's windshield and the 18 recessed bolts that secured the front cover plate (also called the differential opening cover) to the glacis.

The M5A1 was the M24's immediate precursor in the U.S. light tank inventory. Features of the M5A1 were a 37mm main gun and vertical volute spring suspension, in contrast to the M24's 75mm gun and torsion bar suspension. The M24 was longer and wider than the M5A1, but several inches shorter in height.

Even 60 years after its initial production, the M24 still looks modern due to its low profile and torsion bar suspension.

Powered by twin Cadillac V-8 engines, the M24 Chaffee could attain 34 miles per hour on road.

A series of lightening holes surrounds the 10 hub-safety nuts on the M24's outer sprockets. The points of this sprocket are slightly worn from contact with the T72 track.

The sprockets themselves could be removed from the hubs and reversed, so that wear on this expensive component could be evened out. This vehicle is equipped with T85A1 track. (David E. Harper)

As seen with the track raised out of the way, the sprocket hub has circular lightening holes on the outside and elongated holes on the inside. Sprocket mounting bolts protrude through the hub. There are locking wires on the bolt heads on the inner face of the final-drive assembly.

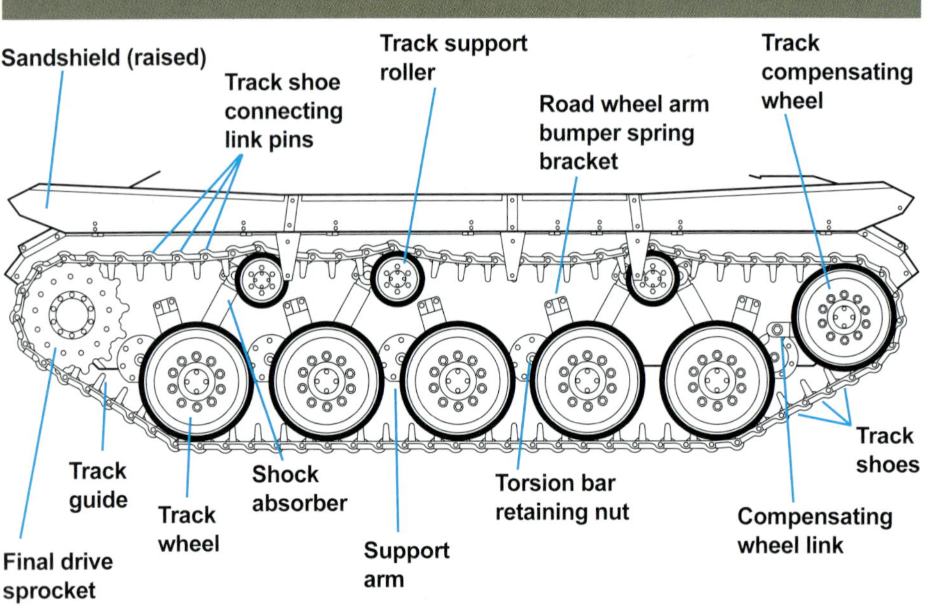

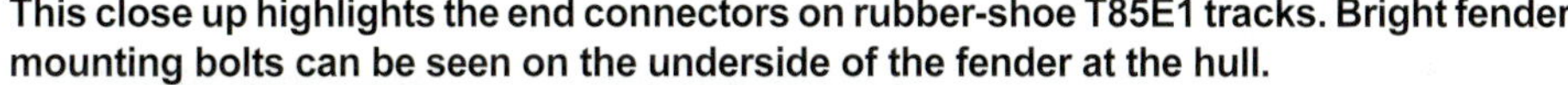

This well-weathered set of T72 steel tracks is deeply pitted and has a heavy coating of rust. These single-pin, center-guide tracks were 16 inches wide.

The 14-inch, double-pin T85E1 track was used on later-production M24s. This photo of the left, final drive shows the chevron featured on the T85E1's rubber track shoe.

This close up highlights the end connectors on rubber-shoe T85E1 tracks. Bright fender-mounting bolts can be seen on the underside of the fender at the hull.

The connecting band of the fenders is visible on the underside. The outer faces of the T85E1 connectors are rusted and pitted, reflecting years of exposure to the elements.

Track Shoe

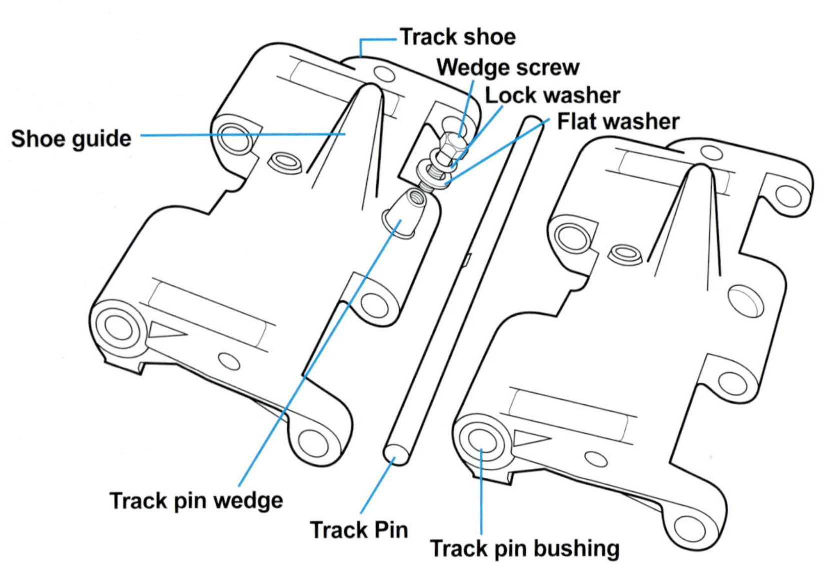

Rubber Track Shoes

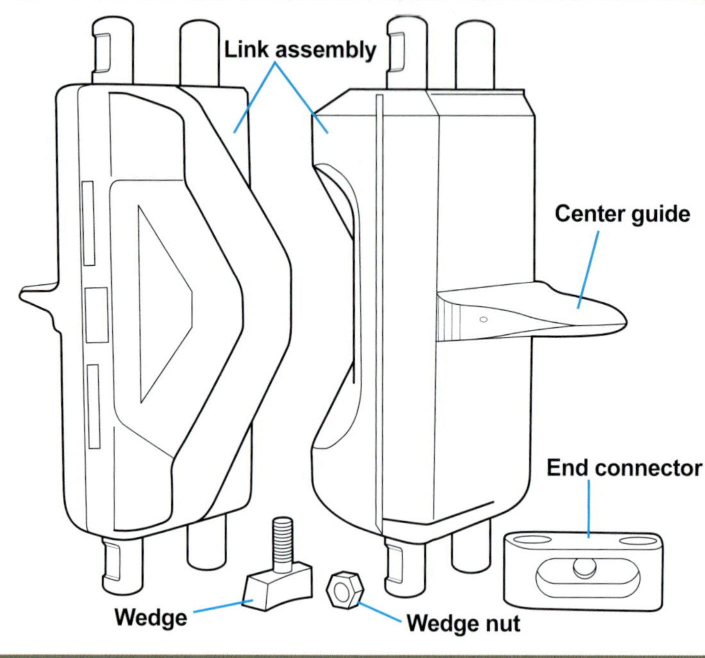

Track Grouser and Ice Grousers

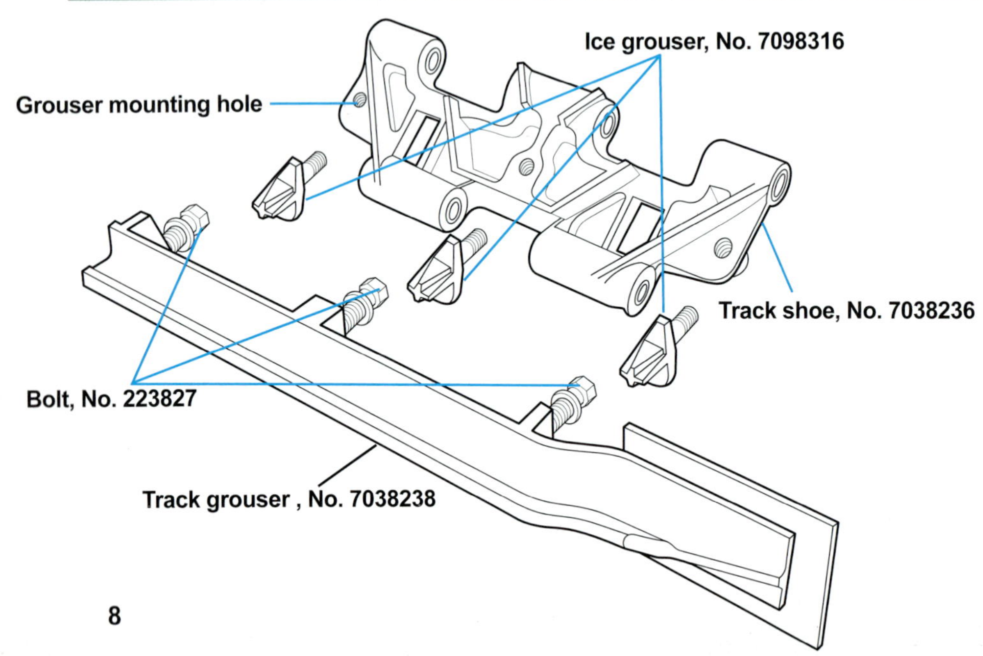

Track Support Roller

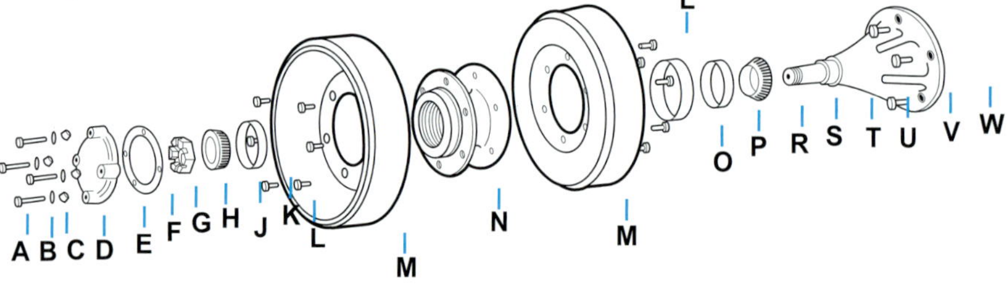

A: Bolt	H: Washer	P: Cup
B: Lock washer	J: Cone	R: Cone
C: Fitting	K: Cup	S: Adapter
D: Cap	L: Bolt	T: Retainer
E: Gasket	M: Disc assembly	U: Oil seal
F: Cotter pin	N: Hub	V: Spacer
G: Nut	O: Slinger	W: Shedder

Bolted to the center of each return roller was a hub cap that featured a grease fitting for lubrication.

The Chaffee rode on 20 of these rubber-tired road wheels, mounted in pairs, 10 pairs per side. A grease fitting, visible in the upper right of the center hub cab, was provided to lubricate the tapered roller bearings on which the road wheels turned.

A return roller and its mounting bracket are seen from the underside, where casting marks on the bracket can be seen. A center guide on the T85E1 track is between the rollers. The "discs," as the return rollers were designated in the M24 parts list, have rubber tires.

This close-up of the front left suspension-arm mounting shows the drive sprocket to the left and front track (or road) wheel to the right.

Oval lightening holes appear prominently in this view, towards the rear, of the rims of a set of compensating wheels. Toward the bottom left is the compensating link mounting.

The left track compensating wheel, or idler, lacks the rubber tires that were fitted to the road wheels. Just visible at the bottom of the hubcap is a grease zerk.

Suspension Arm Assembly

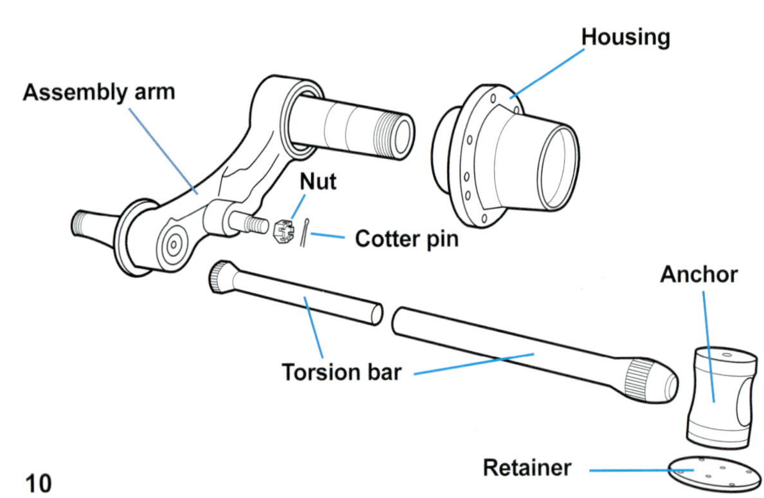

Wheel Arm Assembly

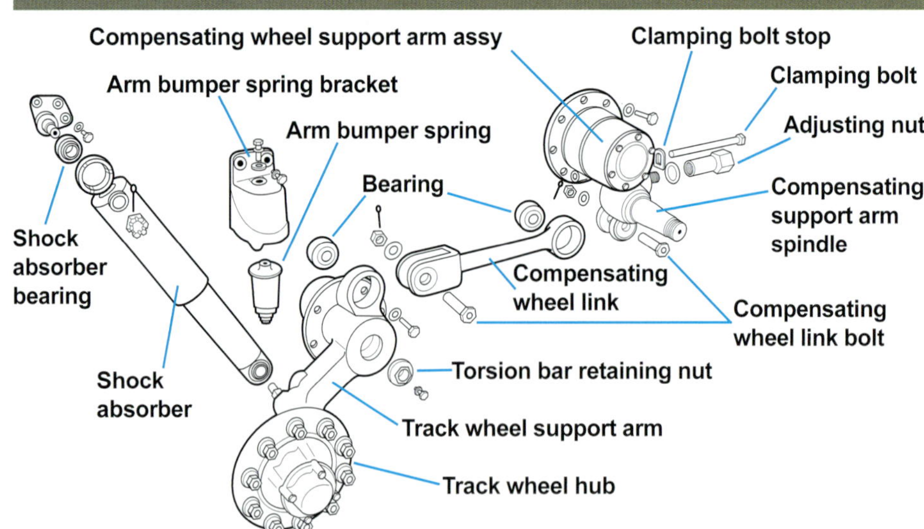

Tipping the scales at just over 20 tons, the M24 was considered a "light tank," as compared with the Sherman, a medium tank weighing about 34 tons.

Above and outboard of the shackles can be seen the mounting points for flotation gear. Chaffees produced by Massey-Harris began featuring these, along with the corresponding front adapters, in January 1945, starting with vehicle #250. The rear adapters were added to the Cadillac-built Chaffees in November 1944, starting with vehicle #1101.

The inner side of the left compensating wheel shows the compensating link and hex tension-adjustment nut.

Early vehicles, like this one, lacked the float attachment points on the rear of the hull. Cadillac began adding them to M24s, starting with vehicle #713 in October 1944. Massey-Harris started to add them in January 1945. (Scott Taylor)

The end connectors of the T85E1 tracks appear along the left side of this view of the tension-adjustment nut.

The compensating arm link, flotation device attachment plate, a part of the towing hook, and a crowbar handle appear on the left side of the lower rear hull plate of an M24.

The left rear towing hook is seen here close up, with the lower part of the flotation device attachment plate immediately above it.

Six large hex bolts secure the towing pintle to the mounting bracket. Cotter pins can be seen on each side of the pintle's pivot shaft.

This side-view of the towing pintle assembly reveals the prominent weld seams that are a feature of the mounting bracket on the M24.

The left tail light assembly is seen here on the back of an M24. Removing the two screws holding the cover to the body of the tail light assembly allowed replacement of the light bulbs.

By the start of the Korean War, an external telephone box had been added to the rear of many M24s. The phone, which allowed accompanying infantrymen to communicate with the crew, was positioned above the right tail light assembly.

The left taillight bracket is seen here from above. The heavy casting in which the light was enclosed was termed a "bracket" in the M24 parts list. Three hex bolts attach the taillight bracket to the rear of the tank.

Casting marks can be seen on the top of the housing of the right taillight assembly in this downward view of the thick-walled bracket. The outboard side of each taillight housing was bolted to the rear fender bracket.

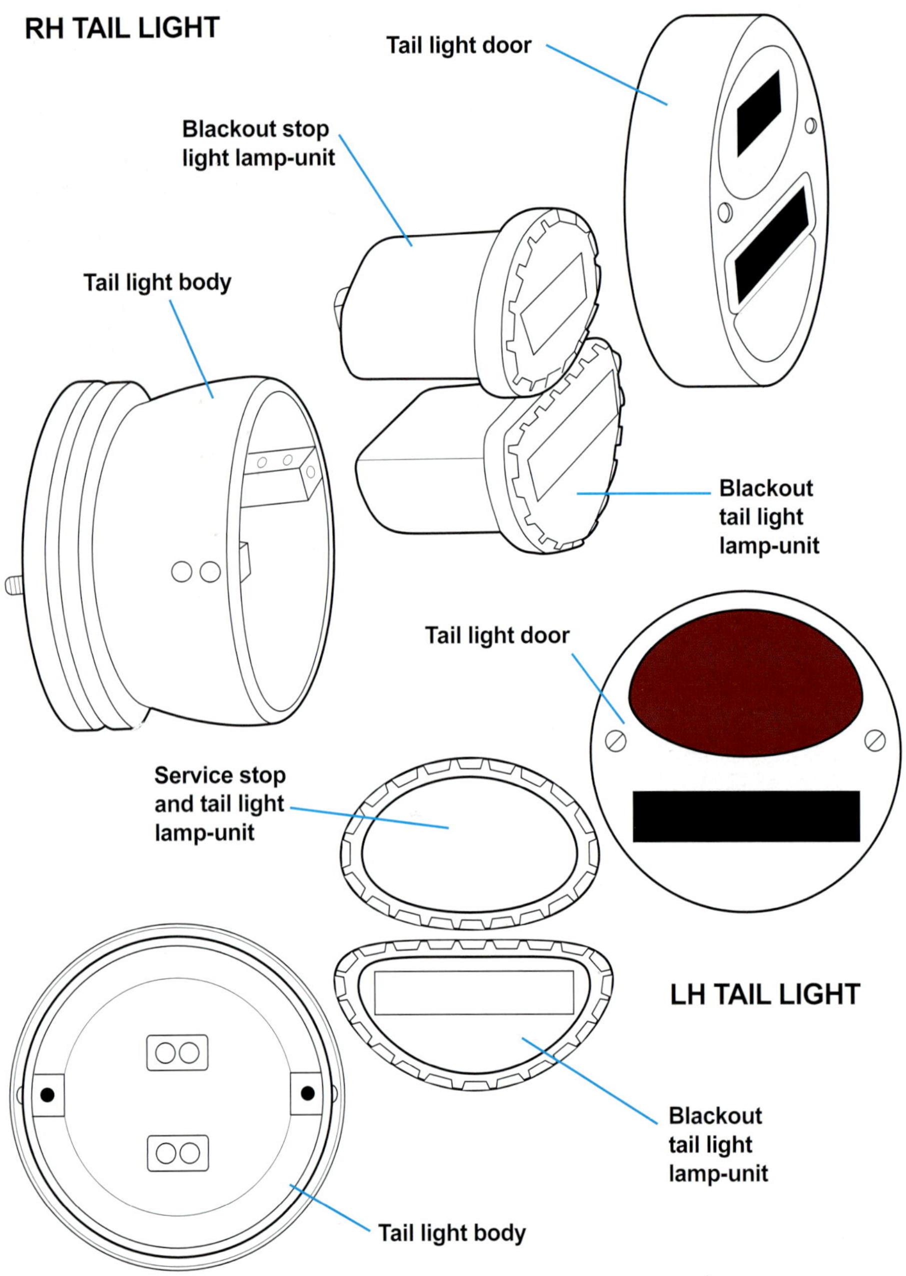

RH TAIL LIGHT

Tail light door

Blackout stop light lamp-unit

Tail light body

Blackout tail light lamp-unit

Tail light door

Service stop and tail light lamp-unit

Blackout tail light lamp-unit

LH TAIL LIGHT

Tail light body

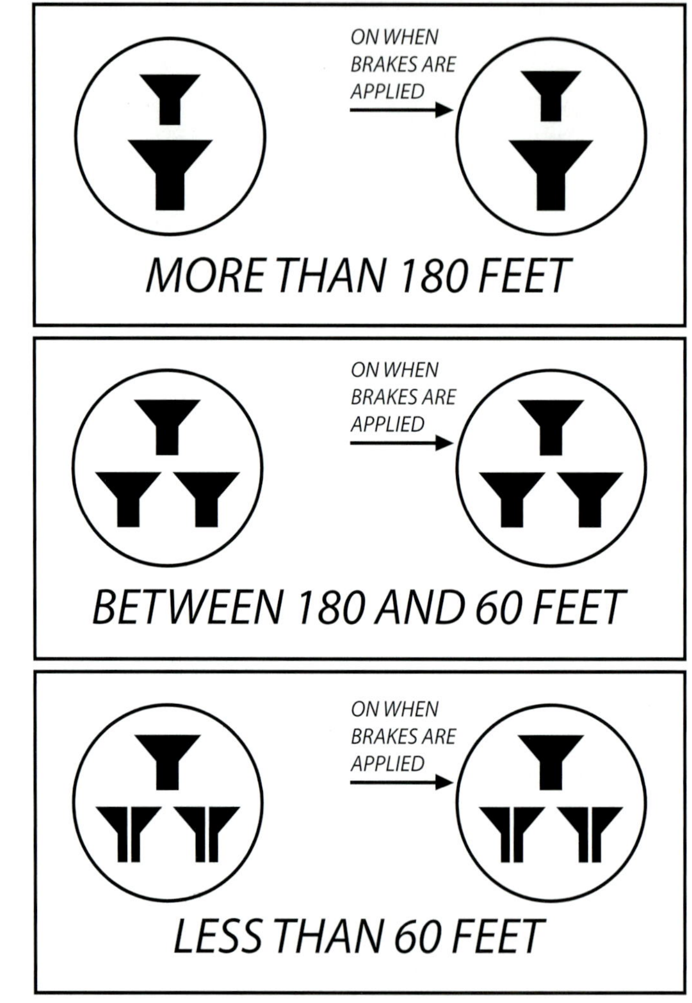

U.S. military vehicles of the WWII-era were equipped with rear blackout marker lights. Rather than illuminate the road, these indicated the position of the vehicle. They were designed to be invisible to an airplane flying at 400 feet or higher. Each rear lamp assembly had two pairs of "cat's eyes" that glowed when turned on. Each lamp assembly appeared as one light when viewed at distances of more than 180 feet; that is, there appeared to be two lights on the rear of the vehicle. From 60 to 180 feet, common column distances, each lamp appeared to have a pair of "cat's eyes," or a total of four light sources visible at the rear of the vehicle. At lesser distances each lamp assembly appeared as two pairs of "cat's eyes," giving eight points of illumination at the rear of the vehicle.

This view of the underside of an M24, looking towards the front of the vehicle, shows the left rear hull floor cover panel. Removing this cover panel and the matching panel on the right of vehicle allows access to the lower parts of the twin Cadillac Series 44T24 V8 engines and Hydramatic transmissions.

The dark "circle" between the outer edge of the vehicle floor plate and the left rear hull floor cover panel is one of two gasoline tank drain covers (the other cover is on the right side of the floor plate). Two more circular drain covers are built into the hull floor cover panel. The cover plate in the foreground is for the engine-oil drain, while the farther cover is for the transmission fluid drain.

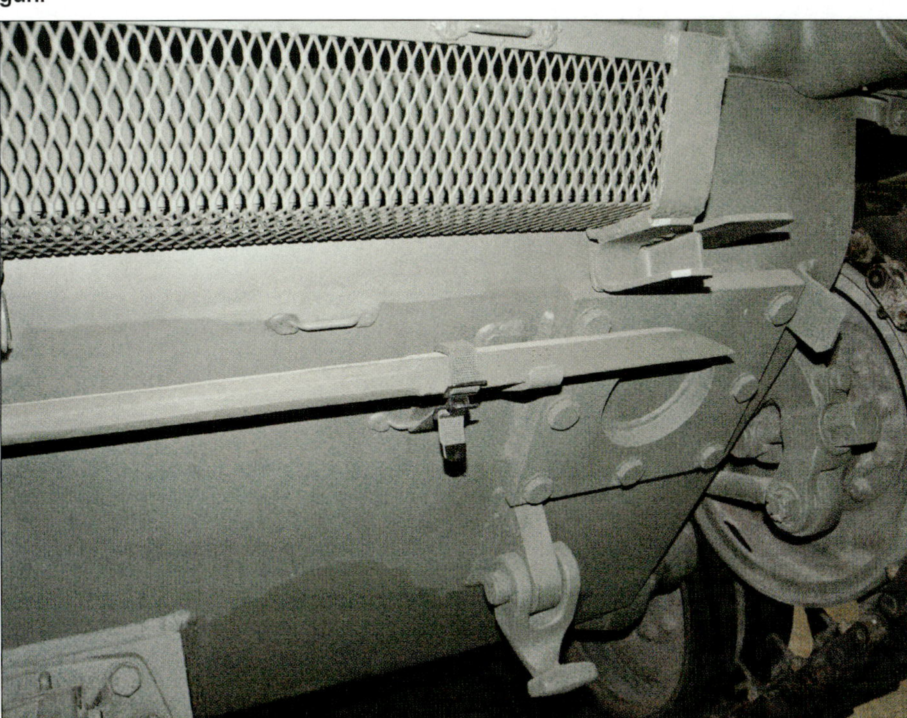

At the top of this photo of the rear hull of an M24 is the steel-mesh-and-frame stowage bin, below which are C-shaped brackets for storing a cleaning rod (missing) for the main gun.

The right-side rear hull floor cover panel with its two drain covers matches the left floor cover panel. Between the two panels is an oval cover for the transfer-unit drain.

A reenactor recreates a typical scenario for manning the .50-caliber machine gun on guard against threats on the ground. The port for ejecting spent 75mm shells is prominent on the side of the turret.

A Massey-Harris-built M24 Chaffee, owned and operated by the National Museum of Americans in Wartime, exhibits the vehicle's characteristic low profile. With proper tension on the track, as here, there was hardly any sag.

The rubber-shoed T85E1 track was commonly mounted on Chaffees during the post WWII-era.

Lubricant has stained the hub caps on the right compensating (or idler) wheel of an M24 and the adjacent track wheel.

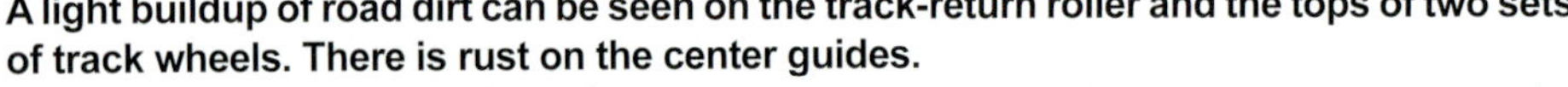

A light buildup of road dirt can be seen on the track-return roller and the tops of two sets of track wheels. There is rust on the center guides.

The center track wheel has a slightly crumpled rim towards the top. Grime from lubricant and dirt is evident around the hub caps of the track wheels and return rollers.

Visible between two sets of track wheels are the pivot end of a suspension arm and the tops of two suspension-arm stop-cushion brackets.

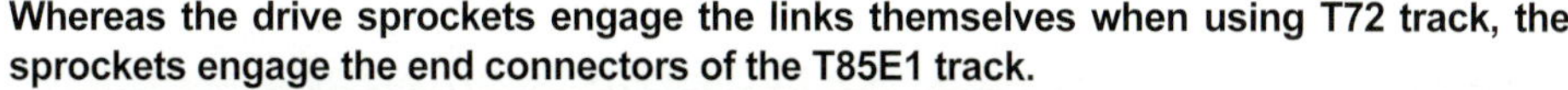

Whereas the drive sprockets engage the links themselves when using T72 track, the sprockets engage the end connectors of the T85E1 track.

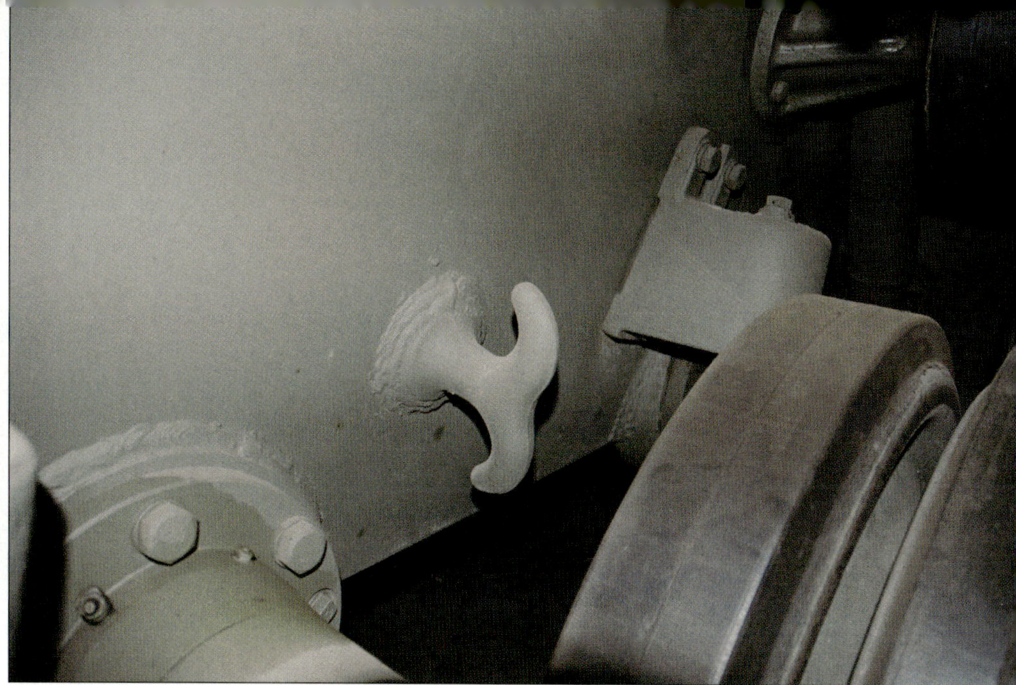

A dual-pronged hook was welded to a base plate on the hull to the rear of the third track wheel from the front.

Final Drive Assembly

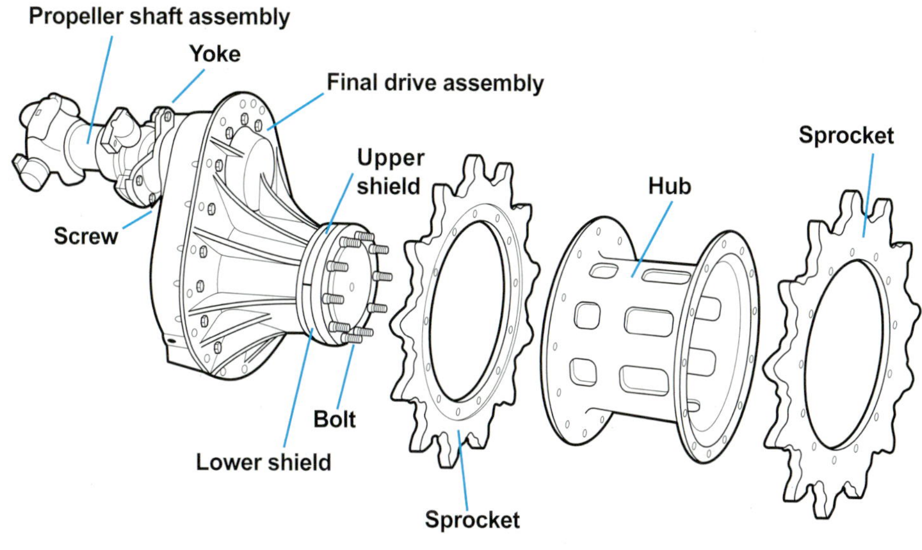

A front three-quarters view of Skeeter at Aberdeen Proving Ground. This M24 has a full complement of sand shields. Made of thin sheet metal, these multi-part extensions were bolted to the fender. In field service, however, some or all of the shields might sometimes be removed, because the metal frequently crumpled or was otherwise bent and damaged.

The M24's frontal hull armor was 1 inch thick, with the upper part being slanted at 60 degrees from vertical, and the lower part 45 degrees. The armor on the front of the turret and the gun shield was 1.5 inch thick.

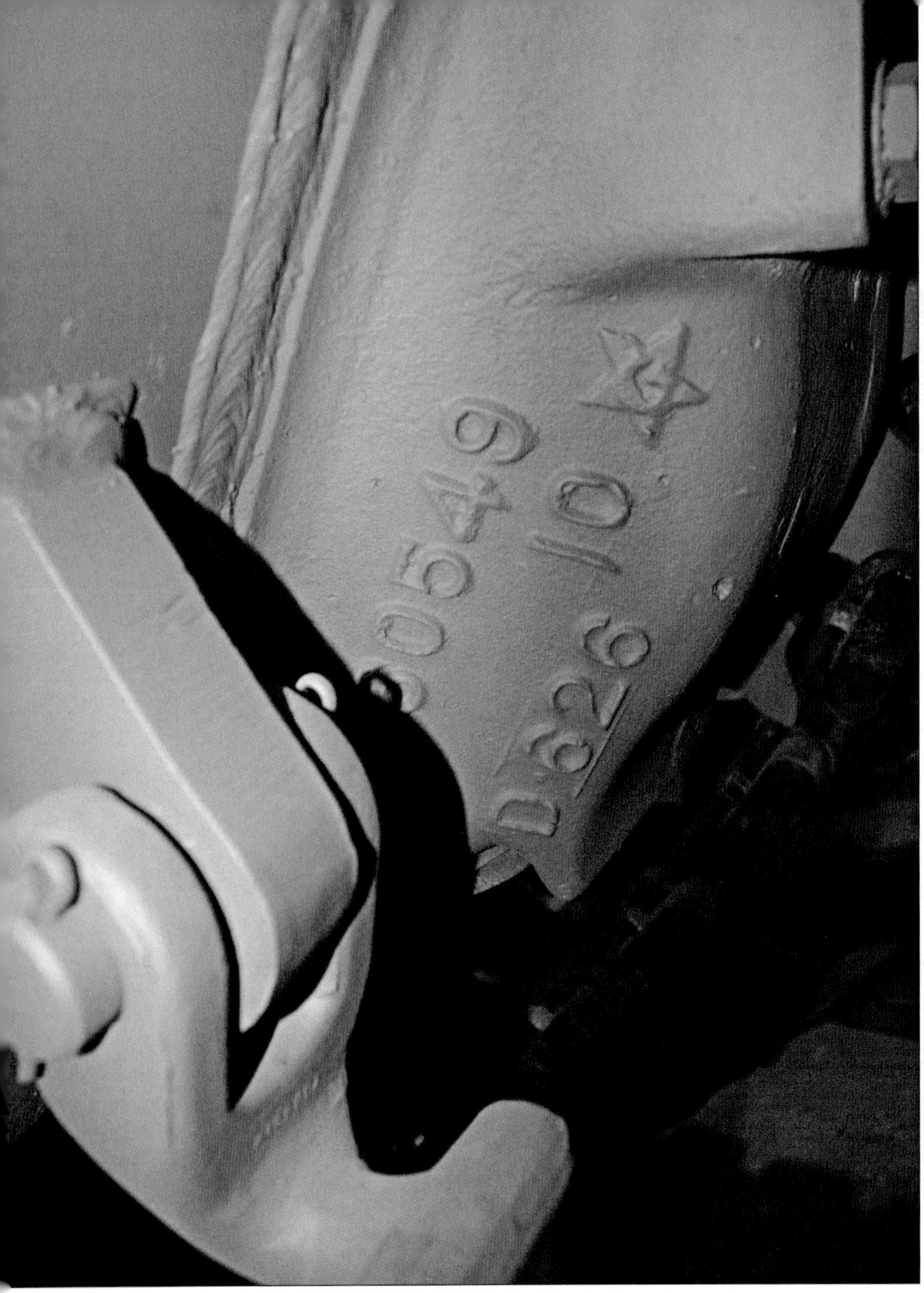

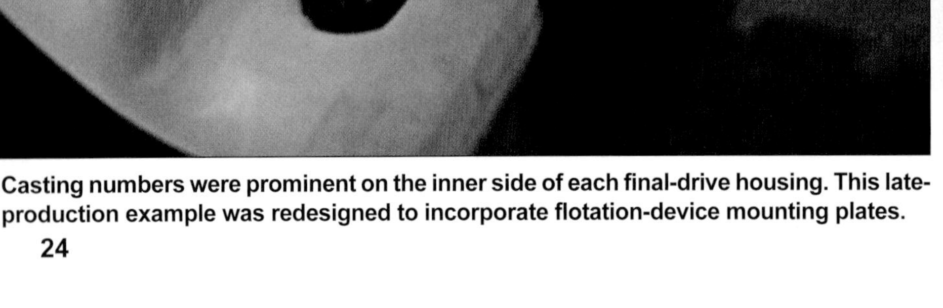

Casting numbers were prominent on the inner side of each final-drive housing. This late-production example was redesigned to incorporate flotation-device mounting plates.

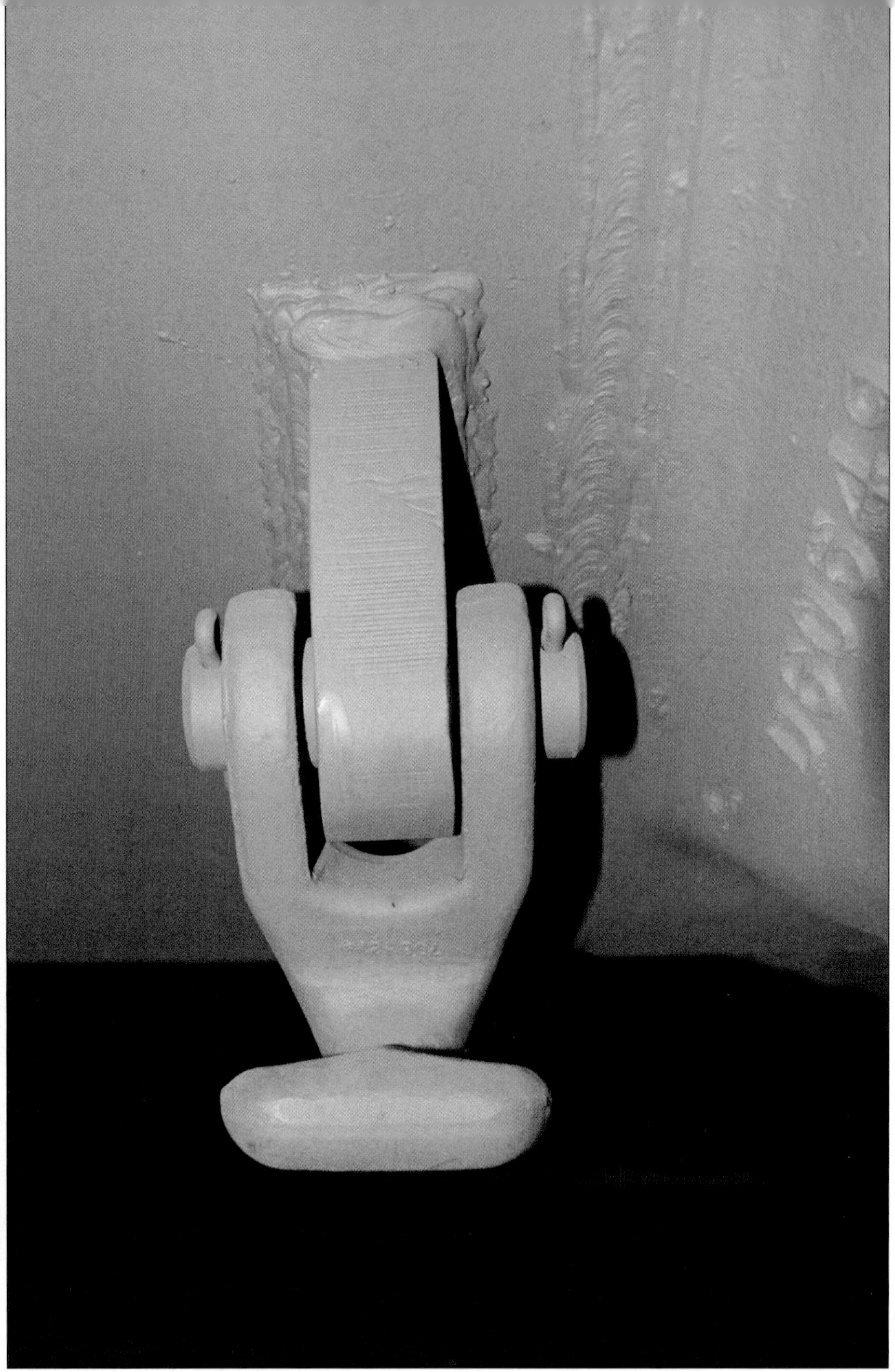

The heads of cotter pins are visible on either side of the towing hook welded onto the left side of the front of the vehicle.

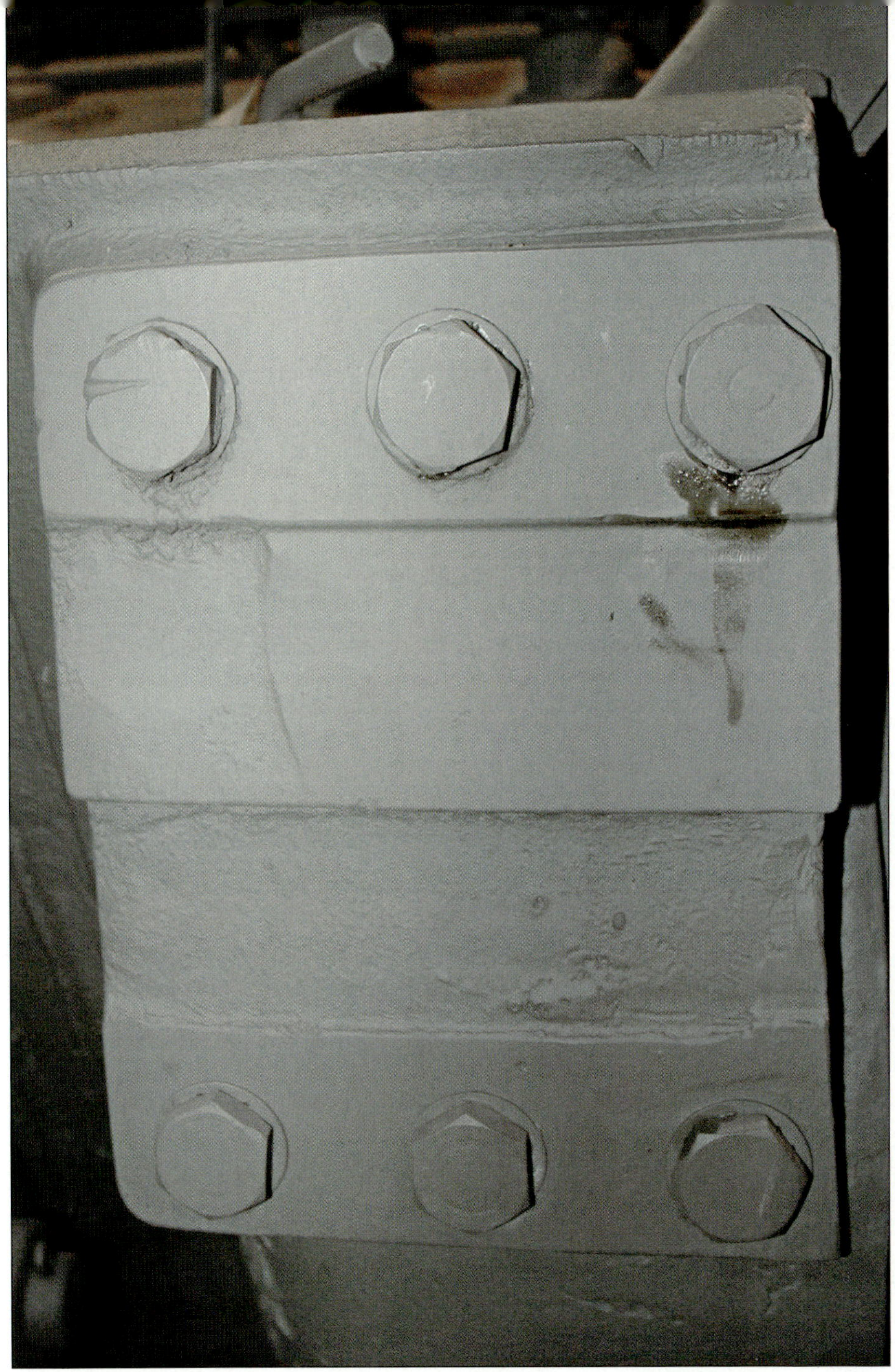

A view looking upwards at the front left mounting pad for the flotation device. Some references incorrectly identify this feature as a bulldozer attachment pad.

The earliest vehicles lacked the float attachment points, instead having only plain armor plate. (Scott Taylor)

Between the right headlight assembly and the front cover plate is the ball-mounted .30-caliber machine gun. This weapon was operated by the assistant driver and was intended for use against infantry.

One of two door latch handles for the assistant driver's hatch (or door, the terminology used in M24 parts lists and technical manuals) is seen to the top left of the headlight assembly and guard, hull machine gun ball mount, and front cover plate.

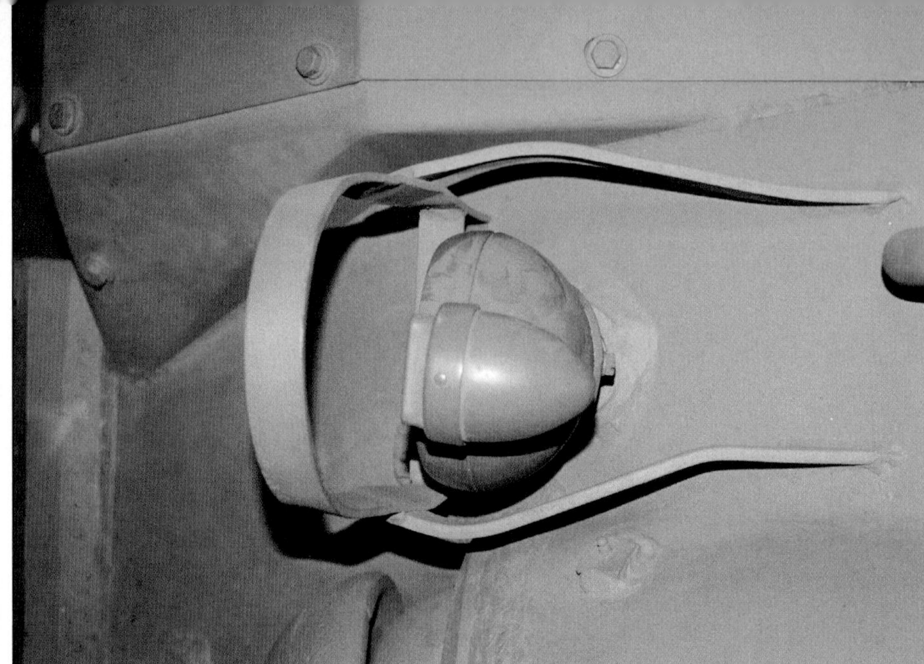

A view from above shows the right headlight assembly, with the smaller blackout marker light mounted atop the headlight. The welds attaching the headlight guard braces to the glacis are in evidence.

The ball mount for the .30-caliber hull machine gun is seen from the side. The outer hemisphere (to the left) of the ball is attached to the gun barrel and moves as the machine gun moves; the inner hemisphere, to the right, is a fixed part of the housing.

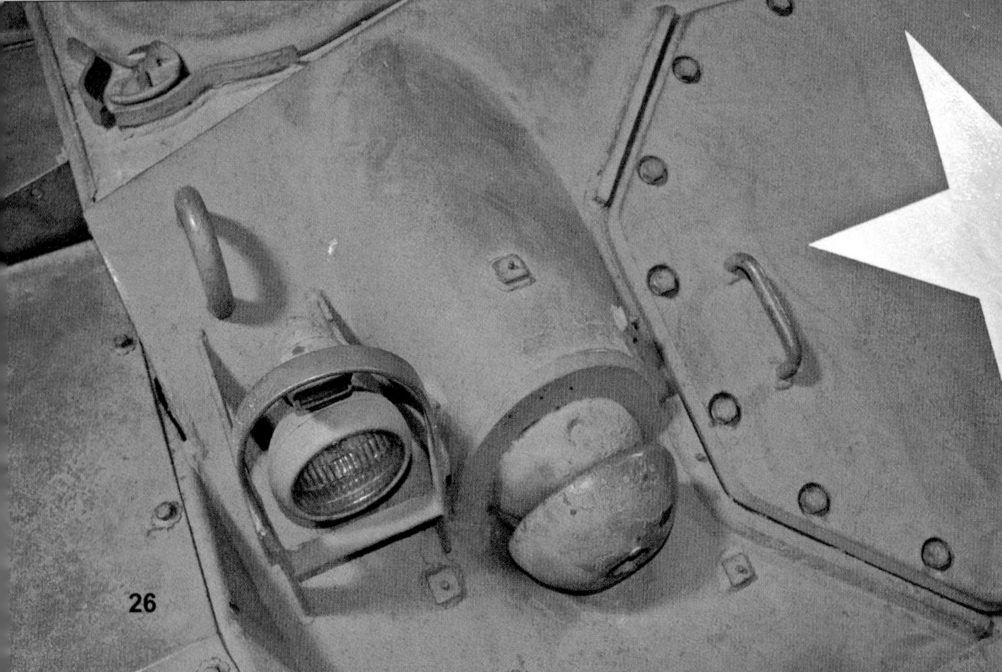

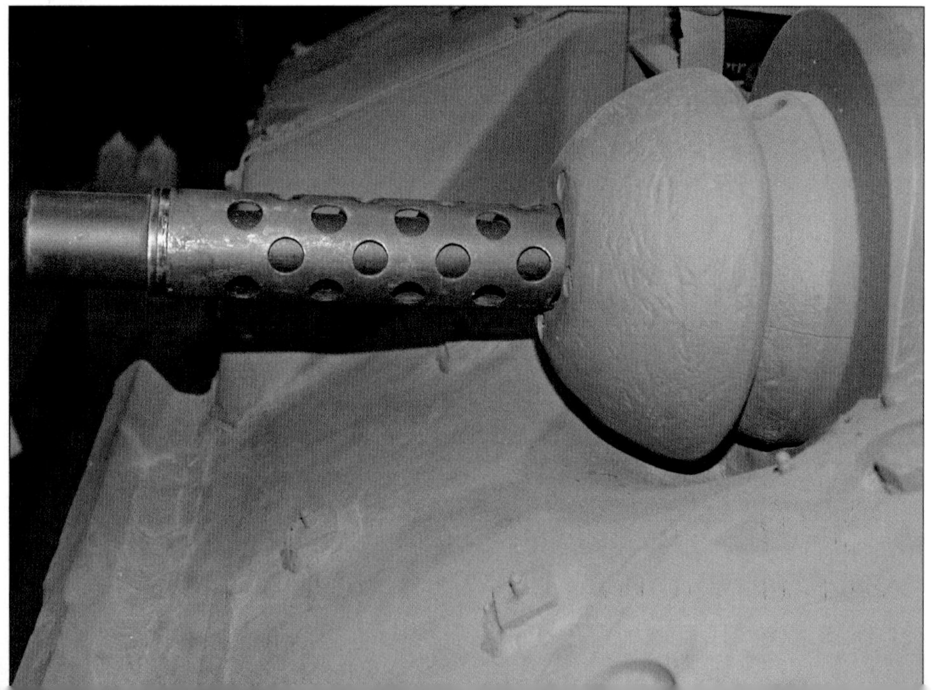

The coaxial .30-caliber machine gun barrel protruded from the aperture in the main gun shield beside and slightly below the main gun (left of the gun, in the photo). The gunner's sight objective was in the aperture on the other side of the cannon and slightly above it. There was a slight bulge in the gun shield below the barrel sleeve.

The left headlight array includes a brush guard, siren (left), and headlight, atop which latter is a blackout marker light. The driver's door is open here and the driver's detachable windshield (which lacks a windshield wiper) is folded-down.

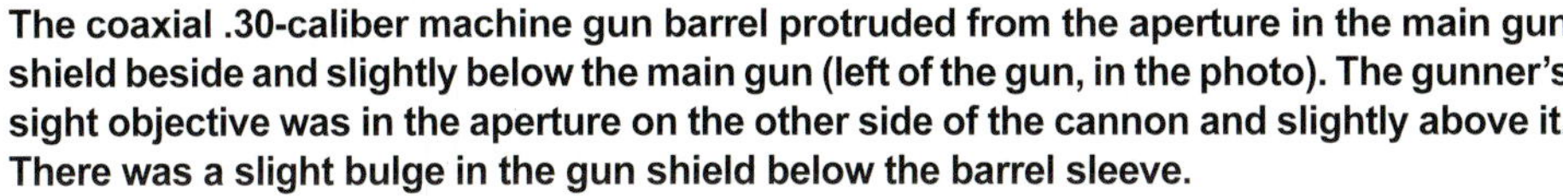

The left headlight assembly is seen here from above. The brush guard brace is bolted to the guard as well as to a mounting stud welded to the glacis.

The main gun shield has a pronounced V shape when viewed from the side. A sheet metal shield attached to the driver's and co-driver's hatches (referred to by the military as doors) covered the large piece of spring steel that assisted in the doors' operation.

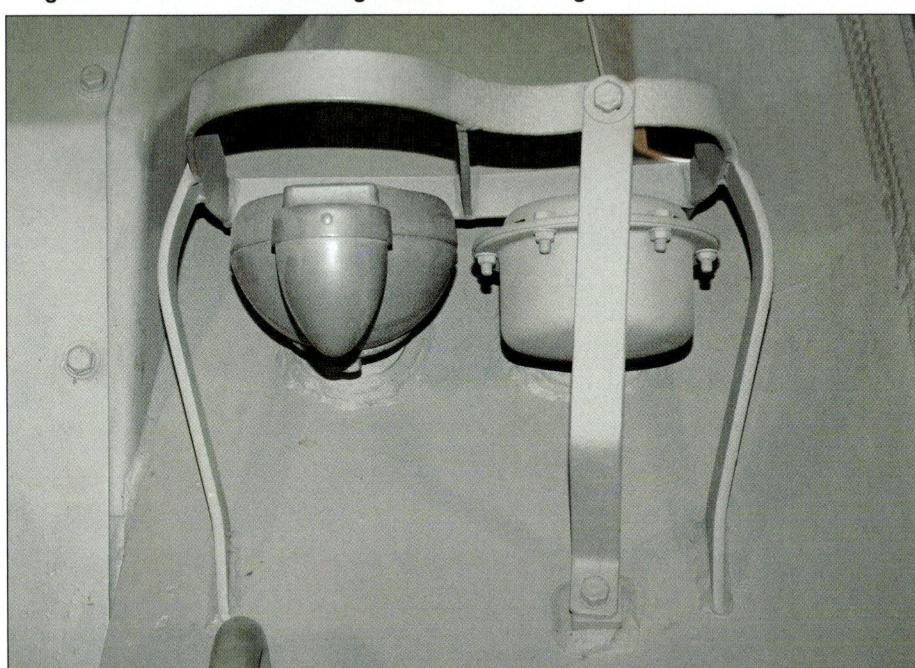

Heavy rubber gaskets surrounding both the door opening and the operating mechanism limited the intrusion of water and other liquids. A guard protects the periscope on this door. (David E. Harper)

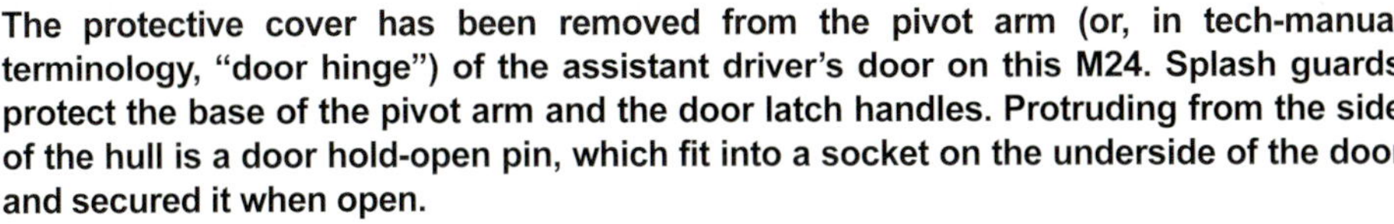

The protective cover has been removed from the pivot arm (or, in tech-manual terminology, "door hinge") of the assistant driver's door on this M24. Splash guards protect the base of the pivot arm and the door latch handles. Protruding from the side of the hull is a door hold-open pin, which fit into a socket on the underside of the door and secured it when open.

The protective cover of the pivot mount on the assistant driver's door is located between the zzopen hatch (below) and the roughly-cast turret (above).

To operate the inboard door latch handle on the assistant driver's door from the outside, the T-bar handle is pulled up and rotated. There is also an extension of the latch inside the forward compartment, so the door can be latched or unlatched from within the vehicle.

A ventilator cover is between the driver's and assistant driver's doors, with the turret behind it and the top of the glacis to the front of it. The word "FRONT" is cast onto the surface. The assistant driver's door latch handle and splash guard are to the side.

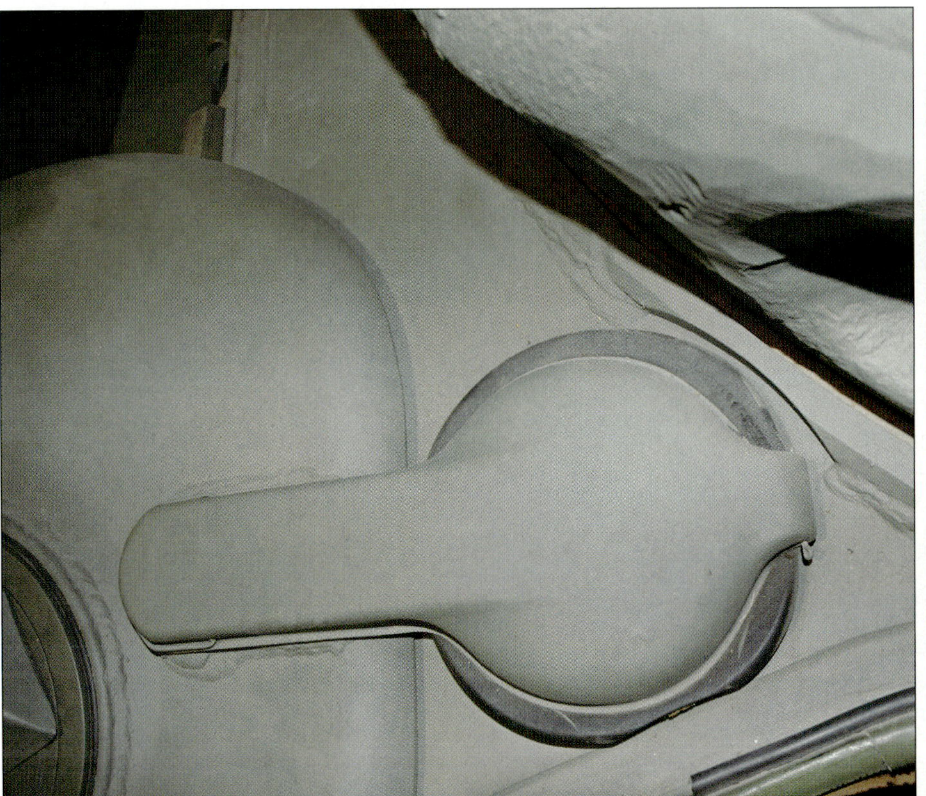

The driver's detachable windshield was equipped with an electric wiper motor as well as an electric defroster for winter use. A removable canvas cover (not shown) could be installed over the driver's compartment and on to the windshield during non-combat wintertime conditions. (David E. Harper)

Visible through the open driver's door are the driver's seat and a white bin that holds periscopes and periscope heads.

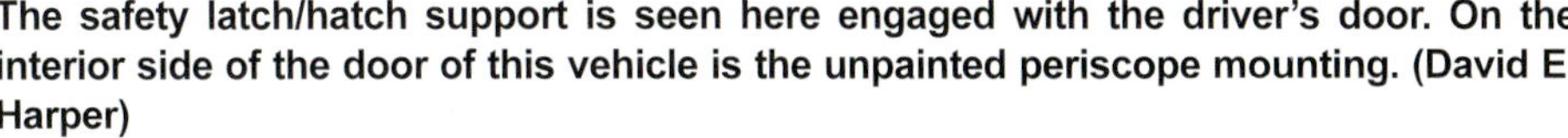

The periscope-head cover on the driver's door was hinged and sat flush when the periscope was not installed in the rotating holder. (David E. Harper)

The safety latch/hatch support is seen here engaged with the driver's door. On the interior side of the door of this vehicle is the unpainted periscope mounting. (David E. Harper)

In this example of an M24, in which a mannequin has been positioned in the driver's seat, the periscope holder on the underside of the driver's door has been painted olive drab to match the outside of the tank.

A Chaffee from the Mullins collection demonstrates the vehicle's maneuverability during an open house for the Museum of the American GI. While designed to be driven with both engines operating, the tank can operate with one engine out, although steering is impared.

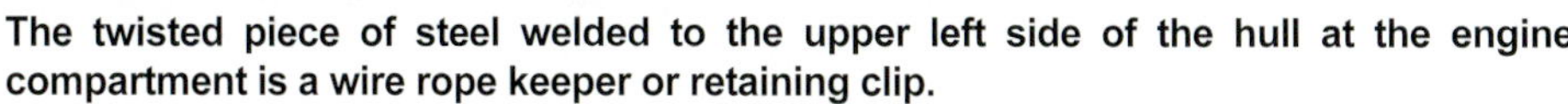

The twisted piece of steel welded to the upper left side of the hull at the engine compartment is a wire rope keeper or retaining clip.

A fender support bracket is positioned underneath the wire-rope keeper or retaining clip which is welded to the side of the hull. At the right of the photo is the end of the protective cover for the external actuating handle for the fixed, internal fire extinguisher.

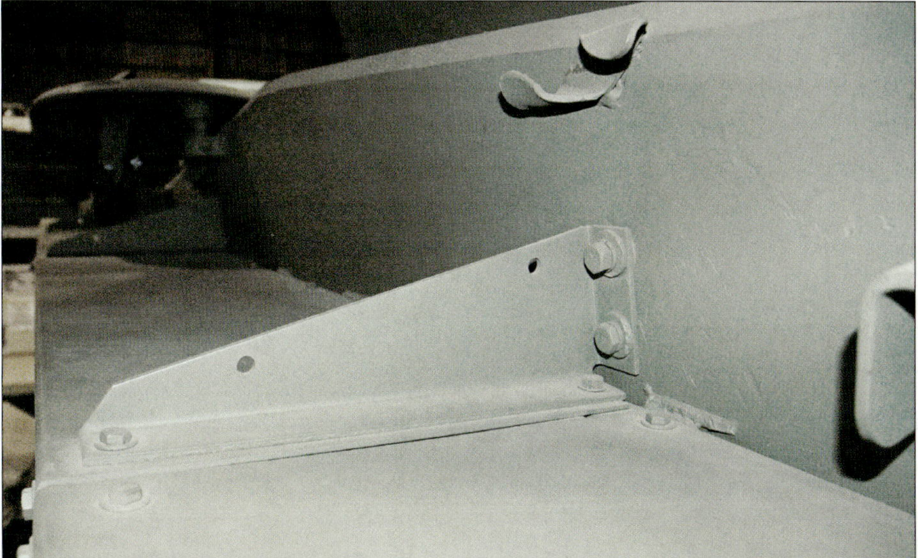

On the left side of the hull is an external operating handle for the fixed, interior fire extinguisher. Beside the handle is the prominent weld joining two hull side plates and the beveled edge at the top of the plates.

There is a spare T85-E1 track on the rear left fender of an M24. The fender support brace is bolted to a stud that is welded to the hull.

There is a turret-bustle storage box on the rear of the cupola of the M24 at Aberdeen. Atop the cupola is an antiaircraft machine gun tripod. On the M24's back deck below the turret storage box are air inlet grilles, the engine compartment door, and an air outlet grille (at rear). The large objects flanking the air outlet grille are fuel compartment vents.

Storage boxes of this design are sometimes seen in photographs of M24s in the Korean War. Details of the single latch on the Aberdeen M24's rear-fender storage box can be seen here.

The radiator cover can be seen just forward of the armored engine compartment door, beneath the bustle box overhang.

Casting marks can be seen atop the left fuel compartment vent (seen here facing forward) and on the hull plate under the handle to the rear of the vent.

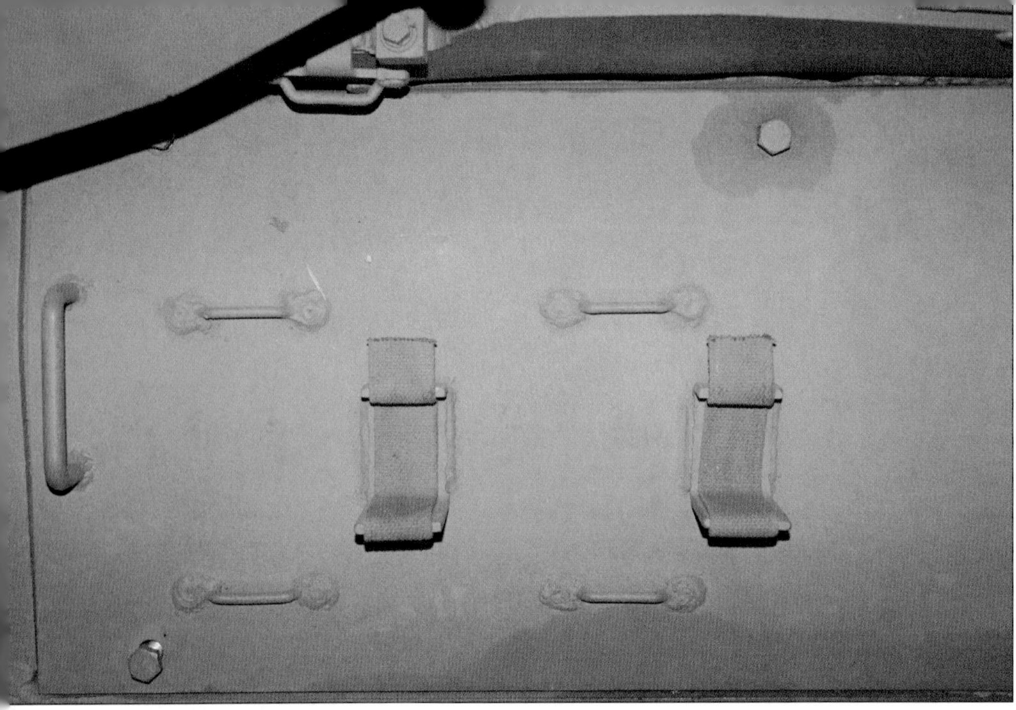

Footman loops were roughly welded to the deck plate, as can be seen in this overhead view of the deck plate located to the left of the air inlet grille.

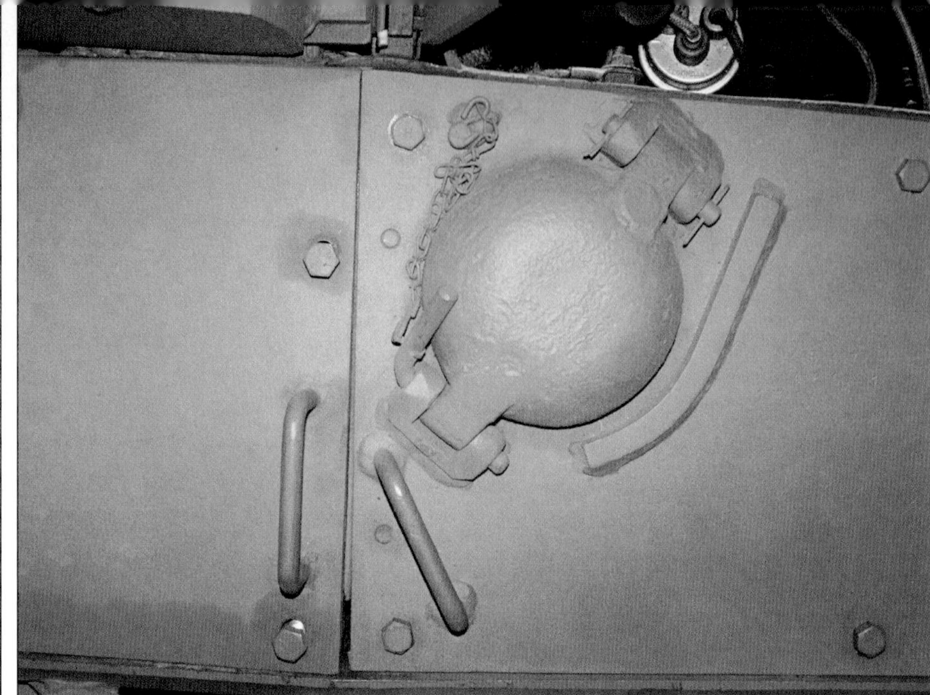

A gasoline filler cover is located on either side of the rear hull deck. This cover is on the left side. A splash guard is welded just to the rear of the cover.

The air outlet grille appears in this view, looking towards the rear of the tank. Protruding from the front corners of the grille are the engine exhausts.

The thickness of the air outlet grille slats and the manner in which they are welded to the grille frame and brace are evident in this shot. The rear of the tank is at the bottom of the photo.

Another photo of the air outlet grille, with the open engine compartment to the top left and the rear of the tank and the bottom of the mesh storage bin at the bottom right. The white object visible in the engine compartment is the left carburetor air intake elbow, which brought filtered air from the air cleaners to the carburetor. (Veterans Memorial Museum, Huntsville, Alabama)

Each Cadillac Series 44T24 engine displaced 346 cubic inches and developed a maximum 148 gross horsepower, or 110 net horsepower. (Veterans Memorial Museum, Huntsville, Alabama)

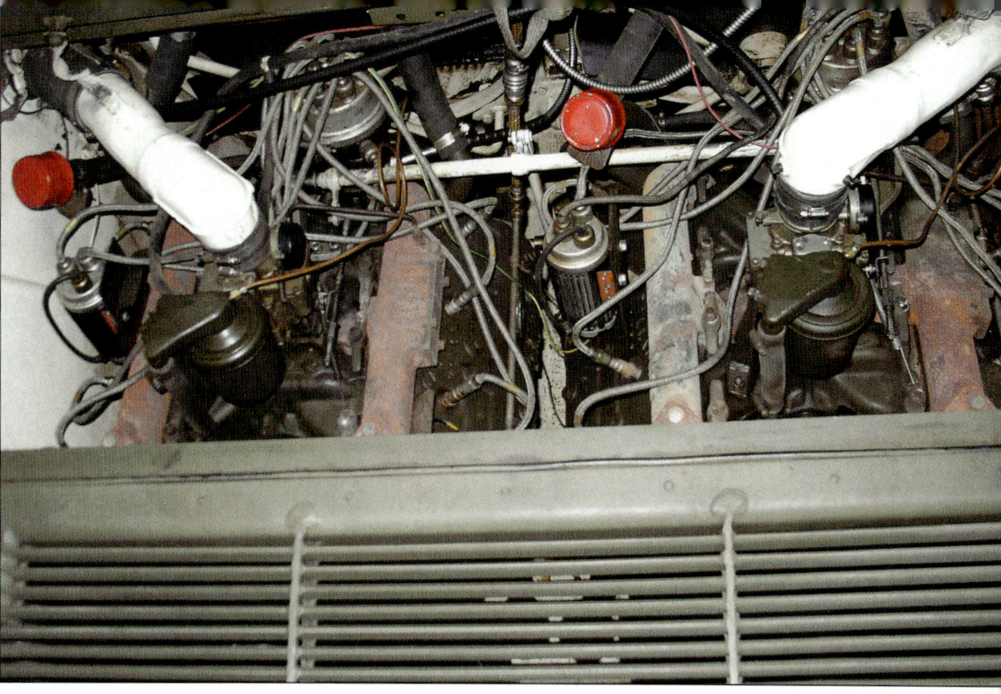

The white carburetor air intake elbows stand out in the interior of an M24's engine compartment, as viewed from the rear of the tank. To the rear of the elbows are the olive-drab crankcase ventilating air cleaners, as well as the rusted exhaust manifolds. (Veterans Memorial Museum, Huntsville, Alabama)

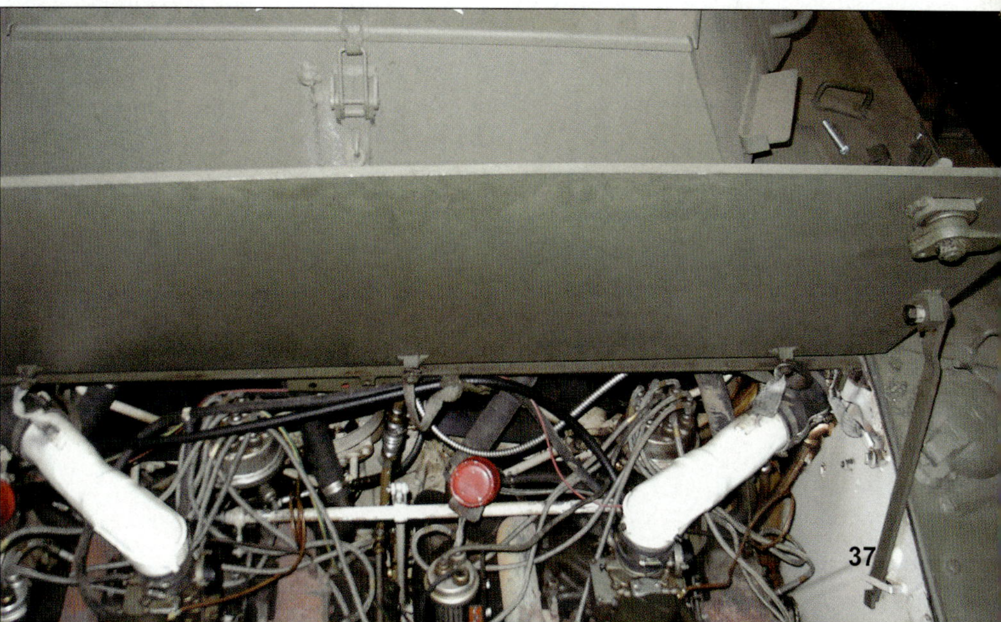

The engine compartment door is held open by a brace on the right side only. To the top of the door is the right latch. The vertical black cylinder with bright cap at the lower center of the photo is the ignition coil for the right engine. (Veterans Memorial Museum, Huntsville, Alabama)

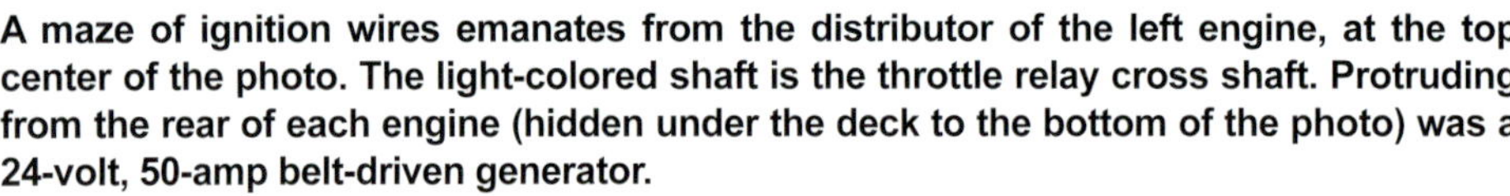

A maze of ignition wires emanates from the distributor of the left engine, at the top center of the photo. The light-colored shaft is the throttle relay cross shaft. Protruding from the rear of each engine (hidden under the deck to the bottom of the photo) was a 24-volt, 50-amp belt-driven generator.

The engine door and air outlet grille have been removed from this M24, allowing a view of the engine compartment and exhausts. The inner surfaces of the hull and bulkhead are well corroded, with only bits of the original white paint showing.

The white inner hull wall and carburetor intake elbow, olive green crankcase ventilating air cleaner, and well-rusted exhaust manifold assembly are all visible in this photograph of the right engine, taken from the rear of the M24.

Among the components in the M24's left engine were (left to right) the generator, oil filter, and cylinder head. The cylinder heads and engine blocks were painted olive drab. The Cadillac V-8 engines that power the Chaffee are similar to those found in the M5A1 Stuart, but will not interchange without minor modification.

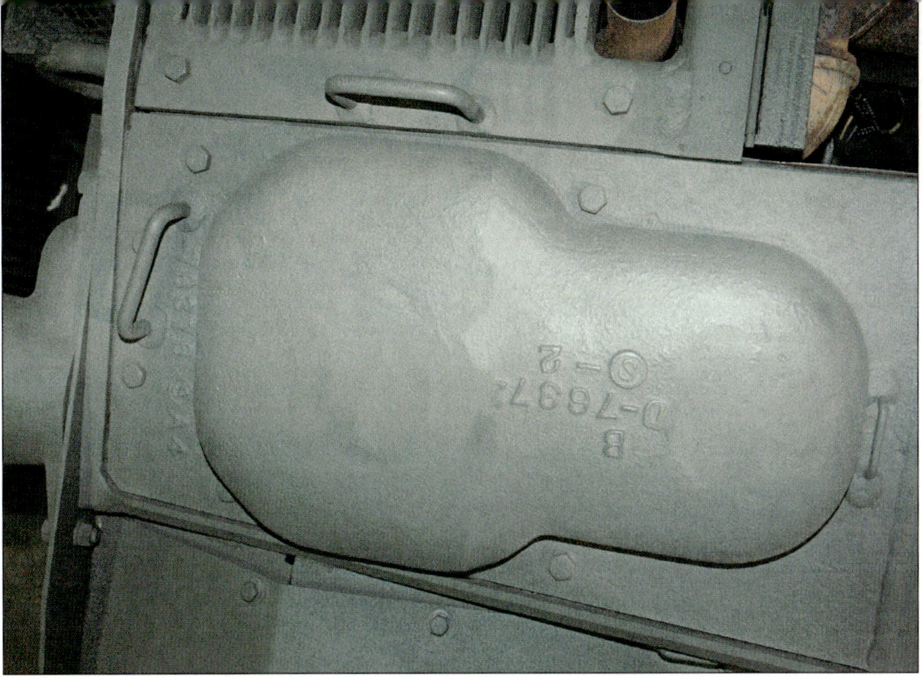

The casting marks are visible on the top of the right fuel compartment vent.

The right fuel compartment vent is seen here from the side.

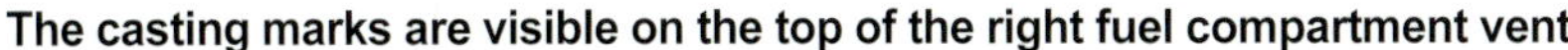

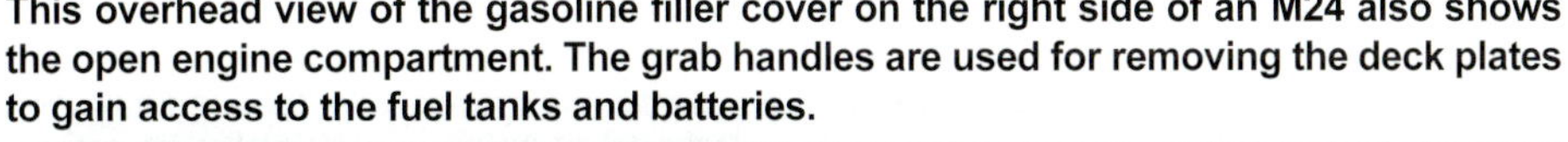

This overhead view of the gasoline filler cover on the right side of an M24 also shows the open engine compartment. The grab handles are used for removing the deck plates to gain access to the fuel tanks and batteries.

This view across the right rear hull of an M24 with the engine door open, shows (right to left) the front of the fuel compartment vent, splash guard, and gasoline filler cover. The fender is at the bottom of the photo.

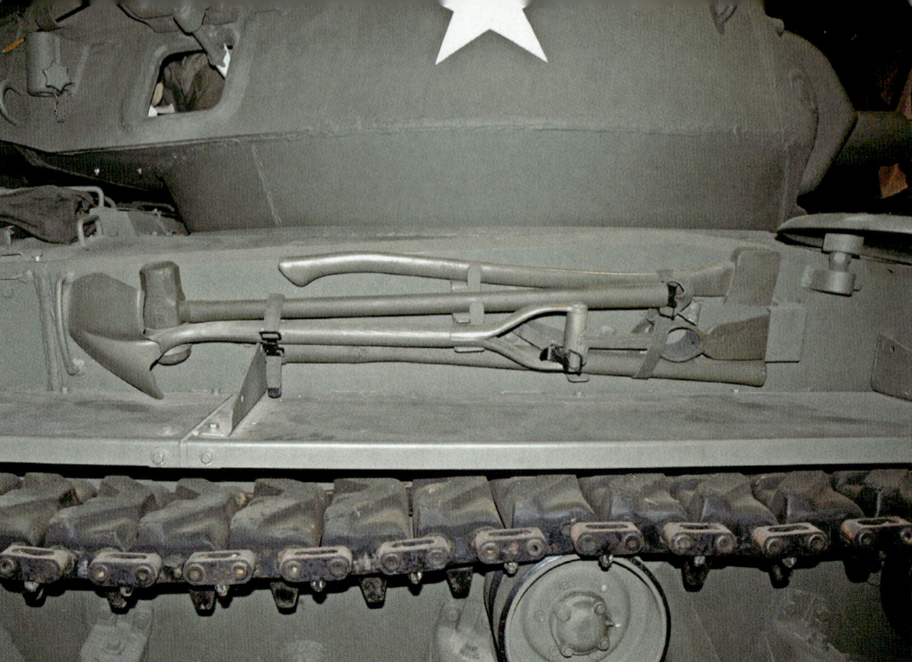

The right rear of the hull deck is seen from above, with the right side of the rear of the turret at the upper right. The engine door is open, at the upper left. At the extreme upper right is the socket for storing the .50-caliber machine gun when not in use.

Tool stowage on the right side of the upper hull included a shovel, sledge hammer, axe, mattock, and mattock handle. The spent-shell ejector port in the turret is open, and at far right, the assistant driver's door is resting on the hold-open pin.

The assistant driver's door is seen close up in its open, secured position, resting on the hold-open pin. The periscope mount, seen on the right, is built into the door.

The knurled knob on the ring of the rotating periscope mount was for clamping the device stationary. The periscope has not been installed in the mount on this vehicle.

Although a light tank, the M24 packed a substantial punch with its 75mm main gun and gave a more modern, streamlined impression than its boxy, under-gunned predecessors in the Stuart light tank family.

There were distinctive and obvious weld lines on the front of the M24's turret. (David E. Harper)

The protrusion at the front of roof of the M24's turret originally housed a smoke mortar. Protruding from the roof at the left is a holder and latch to secure the loader's door when open. There are heavy, rough welds around the splash guard for the roof ventilator cover and the cupola.

The Chaffee was originally equipped with this smoke mortar in the turret roof. These were subsequently removed early in the series' service life. After World War II, radio antennas were often mounted there. (Scott Taylor)

An antenna base has been installed at the right front of an M24 turret where the smoke mortar formerly was located. To the right of it is the mantlet of the main gun, with lifting eyes at the upper corners.

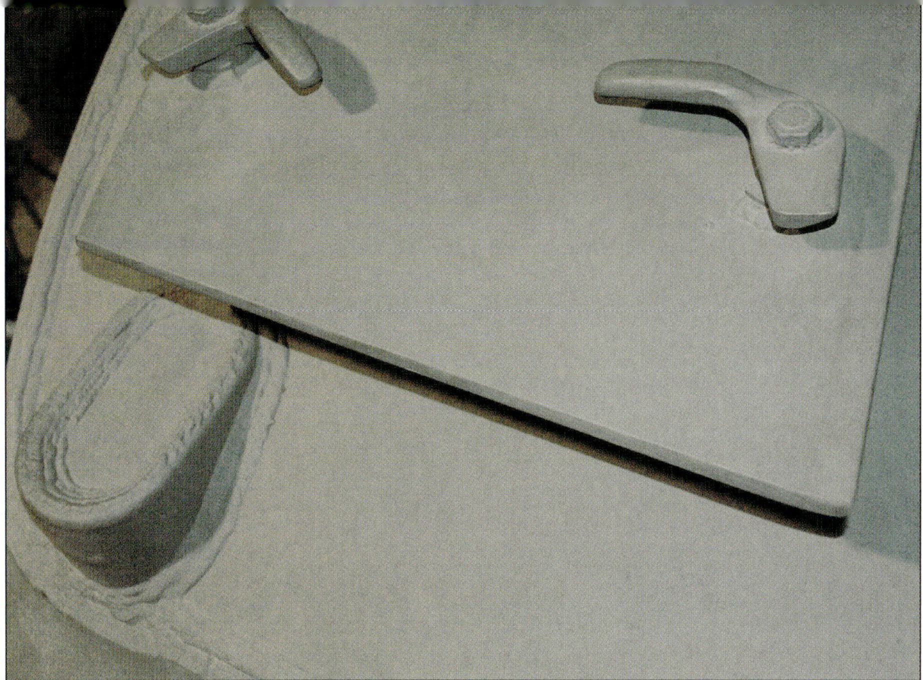

There is a handle or latch on each side of the loader's open door. To lock the door when closed, the loader simply turned the handles, and the latches engaged the underside of the turret roof. The protrusion at the front of the turret lacks an aperture for a smoke mortar or radio antenna base.

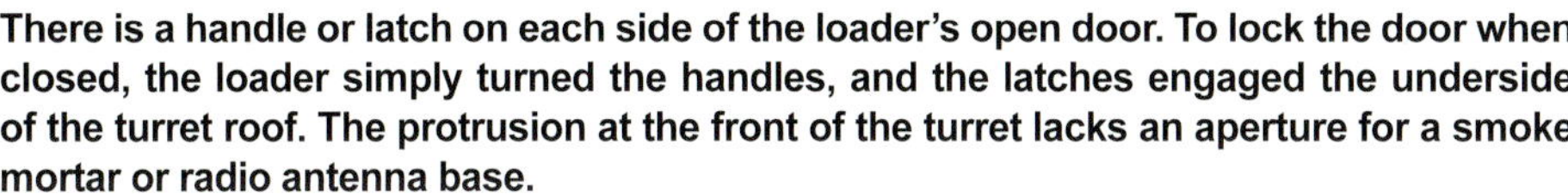

The squared edges of the lifting rings and the pronounced swelling at the gunner's telescope aperture are apparent in this overhead view of the main gun mantlet. The hex bolt in the foreground limits elevation of the weapon.

Casting marks can be seen on the top of the mantlet of the Aberdeen Proving Ground's M24. Behind the lifting ring to the right is the cover for the gunner's periscope. Directly behind it is a sighting vane, which the commander used to roughly lay the gun on target.

The M5 lightweight 75mm gun was the Chaffee's main armament. There is a slight bulge in the mantlet beneath the gun, and there is clearance between the gun tube and the barrel sleeve.

The gunner's periscope cover and commander's sighting vane are seen here from the side. To the right, positioned vertically in front of the cupola, is a socket mount and cover cap for a detachable spotlight.

This overhead view of the left side of the turret roof and the open driver's hatch shows the manner in which the mounting flange of the commander's sighting vane is bolted to the roof at the rear of the gunner's periscope.

The front sight of the sighting vane is a pyramid over which is an arched hood. The commander could see the sighting vane through the left side of the front vision block in his cupola.

Details of the spotlight mount and cap, with its retaining chain, oriented toward the front of the turret.

When the spotlight was installed on its mount, it could be operated manually from outside of the turret, or remotely, using a handle with gears inside the turret.

On the left side of the turret is a radio antenna mount. Early-production M24s had a simple antenna mount, welded from steel plates and mounted lower on the side of the turret.

Heavy but neat double weld lines secure the antenna mount to the turret in this view of the side antenna mount and base and the hinge of the cupola door.

The hinges of the storage box and the tripod mount for the .50-caliber machine gun on the Aberdeen M24 are seen here from the left rear. Light-duty hinges are welded to the sheet-metal box cover. The travel lock for supporting the machine gun barrel when not in use is swung down to the side.

The hinge of the turret storage box is locked by a simple clip, secured to the box by a retaining chain.

The steel bracket welded to the right rear of the turret was for storing a machine gun with ammunition box. The box rested on a flange and was secured in place by a retaining strap running through footman loops under and above the bracket.

The knurled locking knob of the travel lock for the .50-caliber machine gun is at the top in this photograph that provides an overhead view of the turret storage box cover at the rear of the M34 turret.

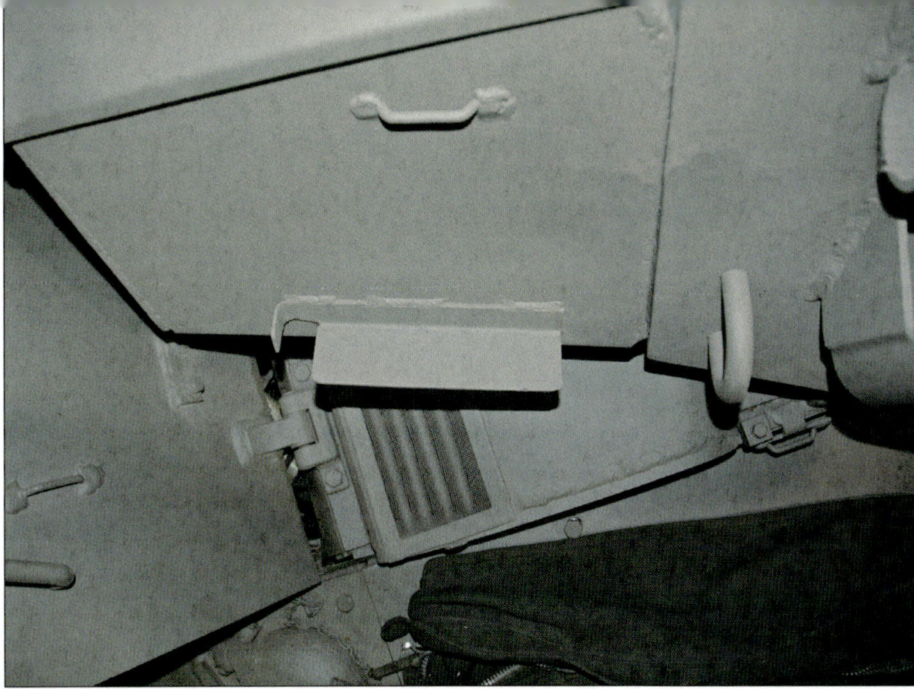

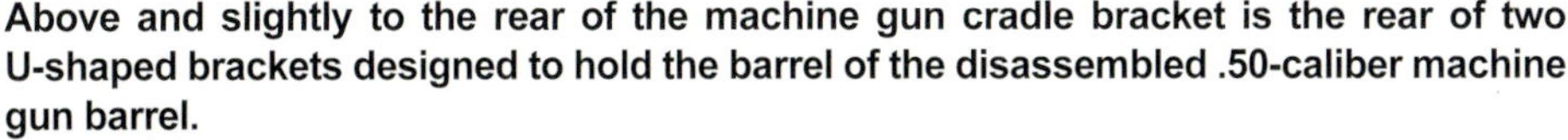

This overhead view of the right rear of the turret and turret storage box reveals details of the .50-caliber ammunition box storage bracket. To the left is the open engine compartment door.

Above and slightly to the rear of the machine gun cradle bracket is the rear of two U-shaped brackets designed to hold the barrel of the disassembled .50-caliber machine gun barrel.

There are storage brackets for the .50-caliber machine gun on the rear of the right side of the turret. The machine gun cradle and pintle assembly would slip into the socket at the center of the photo; the knurled knob would lock the pintle in place.

The .50-caliber machine gun cradle and pintle are stored in the travel position. The square plate with side flanges is the mounting plate for the tray that holds the .50-caliber ammunition box.

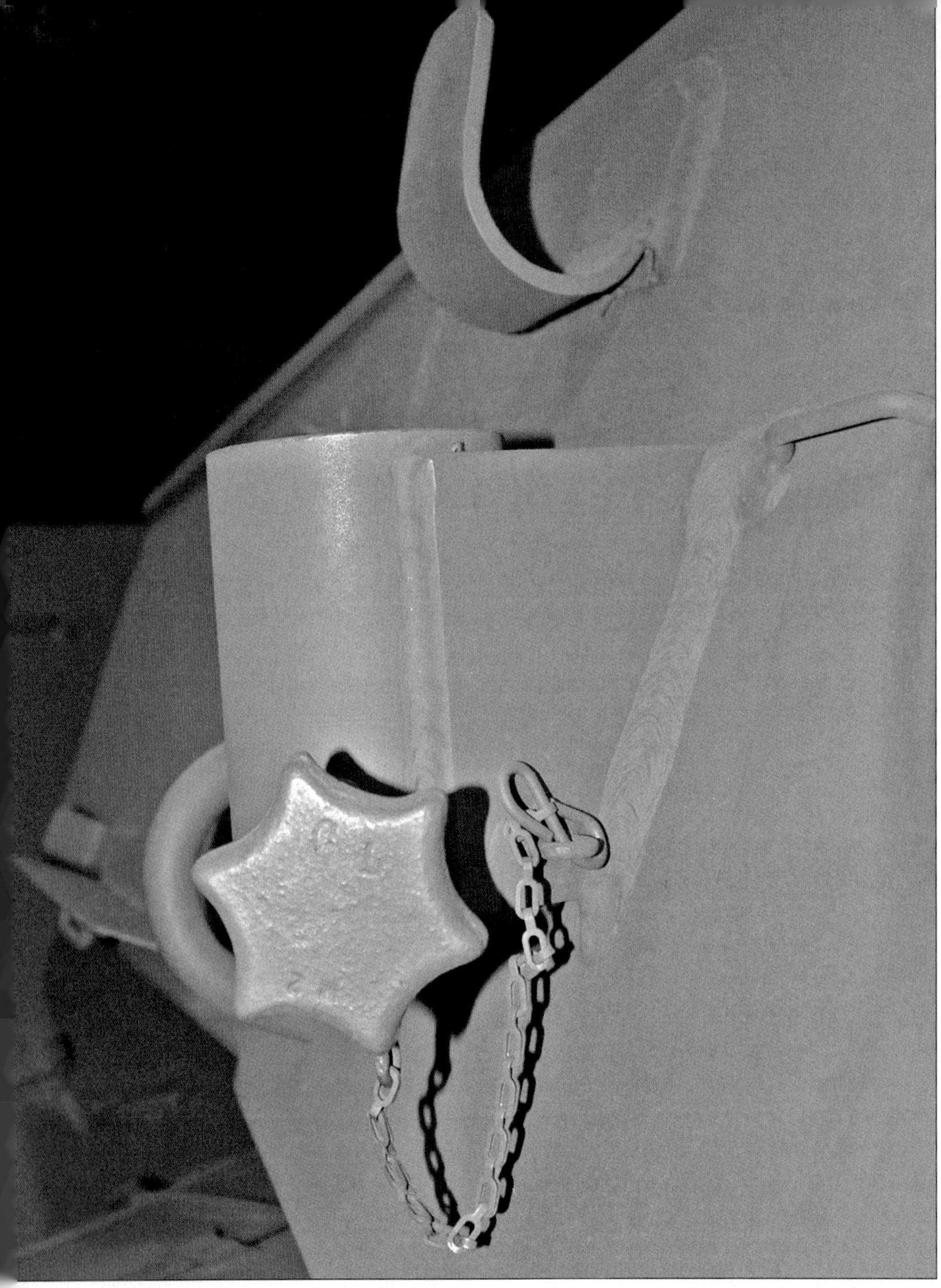

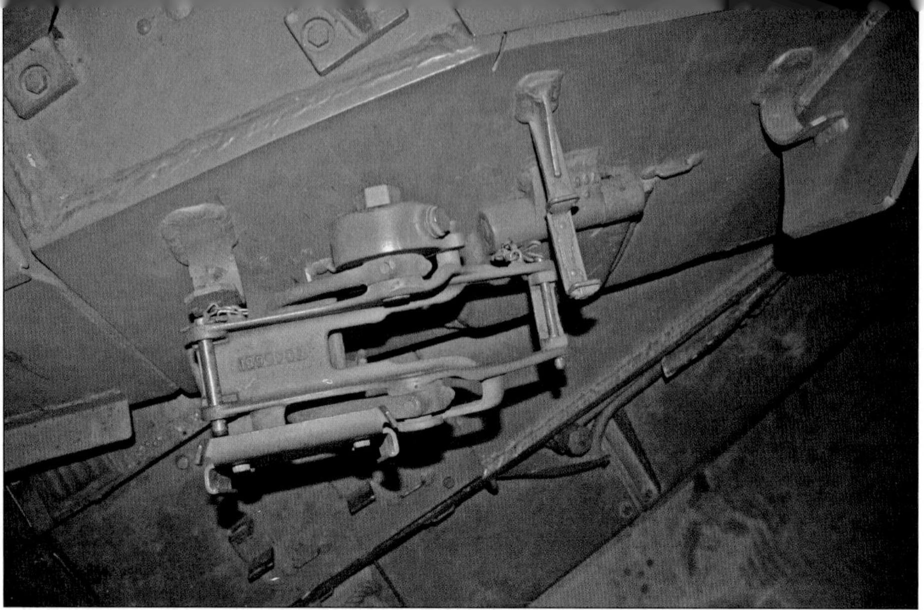

The machine gun cradle and pintle stored in the travel position are seen here from above. During transit or when it was unnecessary to have the machine gun ready for immediate use, the receiver would be stored in the cradle, on the travel bracket. The bracket jutting out to the right of the gun cradle would secure the rear of the gun's receiver.

Machine Gun Mount

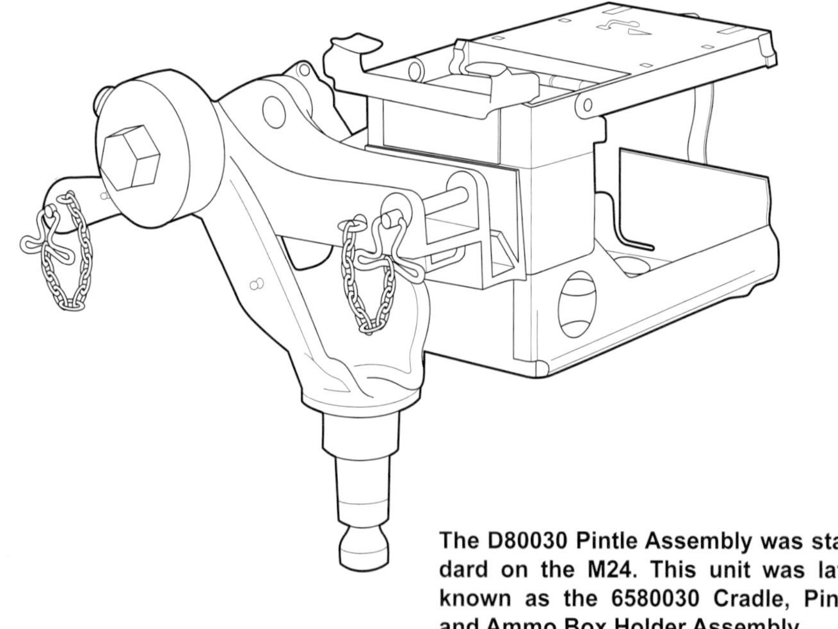

The D80030 Pintle Assembly was standard on the M24. This unit was later known as the 6580030 Cradle, Pintle and Ammo Box Holder Assembly.

The storage socket for the .50-caliber machine gun cradle is mounted to the turret on two welded plates. The retaining chain kept the locking knob from getting lost if it was unscrewed all the way out.

This overhead view reveals the that the U-bracket has been tack welded to the protective armor plate on the turret. Rubber weather gaskets are visible on the inner rim of the loader's hatch.

A casting mark can be seen on the surface of the hinge of the shell-ejector door when the assembly is viewed from overhead. Above the shell-ejector door is the .50-caliber machine gun receiver bracket, to which a canvas webbing pad has been fitted.

A view into the open spent-shell ejector port gives a good sense of the thickness of the door and the turret wall at that point, and the manner of construction of the splash guard: a U-shaped steel bar heavily welded to the turret. The large protrusion under the inside of the -door is the lug for the operating arm.

The inside of the door features a rough-cast inner area with prominent casting marks, and smooth-finished outer rim.

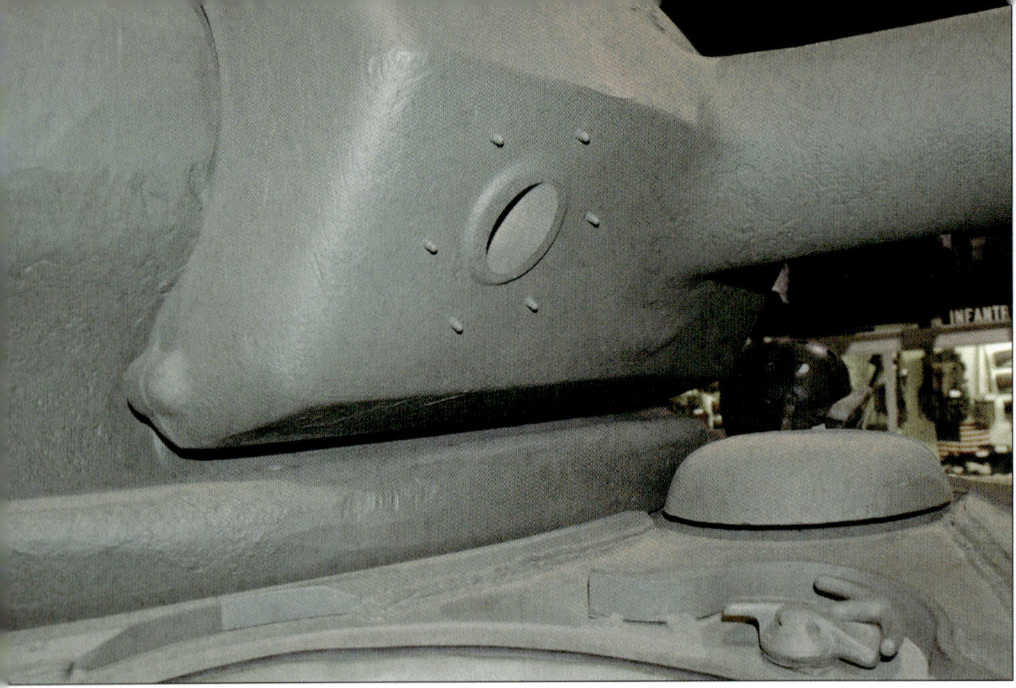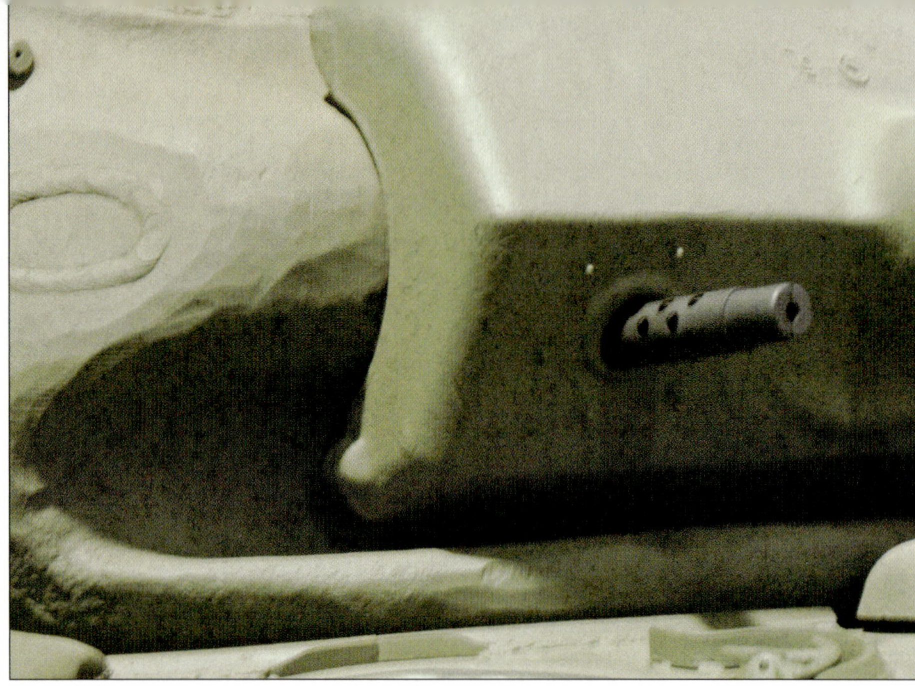

The varied surface details of the turret and mantlet, from grind marks and pitted surfaces to fairly smooth sections, are evident in this photo. A dust cover could be snapped on the six studs surrounding the machine gun aperture.

There was considerable variation in the texture of the casting of the turret from one vehicle to another. This M24 turret has a particularly rough finish. By contrast, the surface of the mantlet is relatively smooth.

Casting marks on the upper center of the mantlet are upside down, as viewed from the front of the tank.

The weld lines of the roof-to-side joint of the turret and around the gunner's periscope mount are evident in this photo of Aberdeen Proving Ground's M24.

Around the inner rim of the cupola door is an azimuth scale, with a pointer to the left. As the commander rotated the center section of the door, he could determine the bearing at which he was viewing an object through the periscope. The round knob to the right of the center section locked the race. The door latch and latch handle are at the top of the door.

There is a casting mark on the cupola between two of its six vision blocks. A lifting handle and position for a periscope can be seen atop the cupola door. This center part was mounted on a race, so it could be rotated, allowing the tank's commander a 360-degree view through the periscope. (David E. Harper)

The square plate with four hex bolts is a cover for an aperture for mounting a British VHF "B" antenna. A roof-joint weld line intersects the plate.

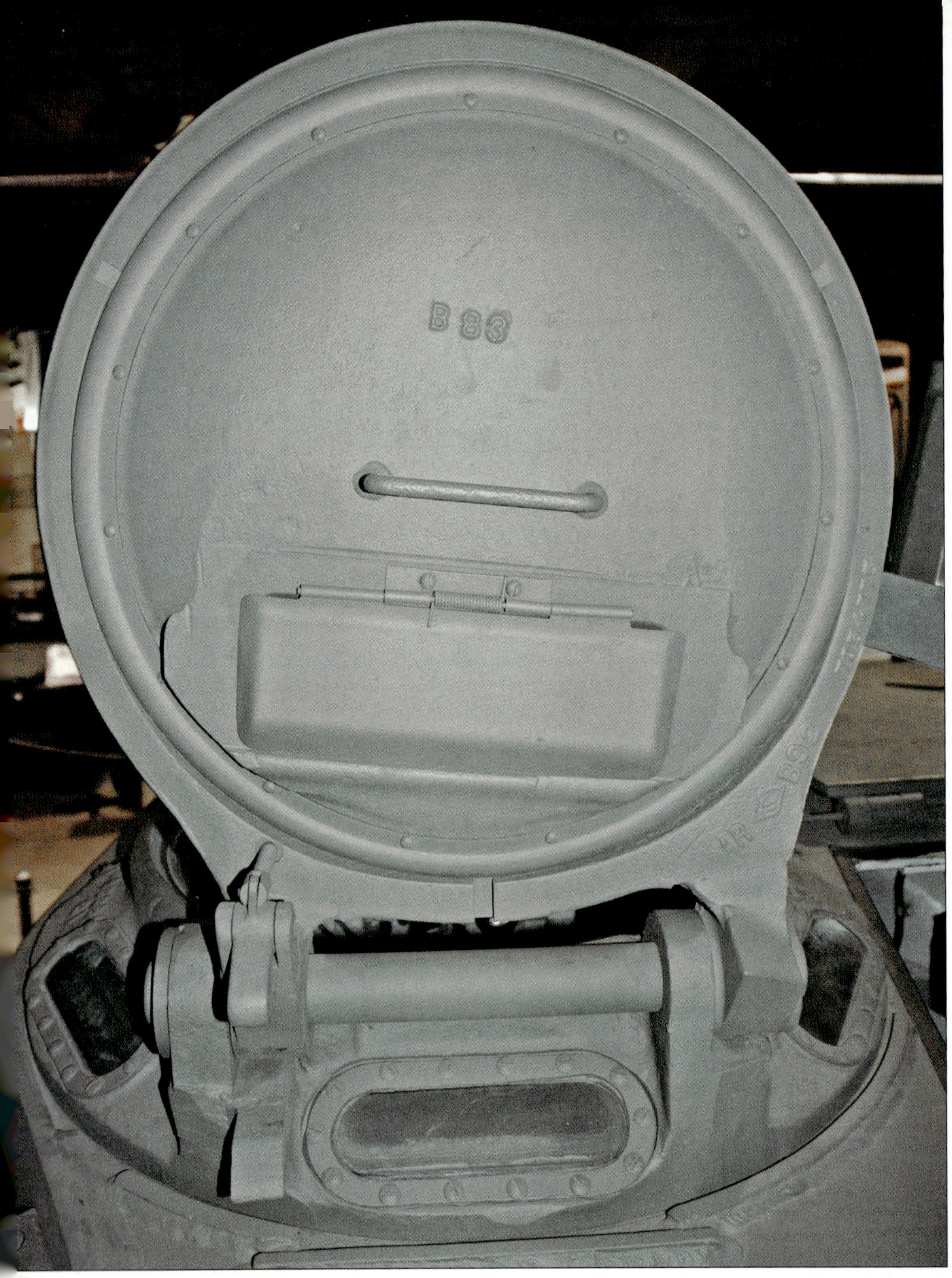

An iron sight was mounted forward of the commander's cupola and just behind the gunner's periscope on the turret roof.

The steel rod running through the hinges of the loader's door is a torsion bar, which assisted with the manual lifting of the door. The .50-caliber machine gun tripod is bolted to the roof of the turret next to the loader's door. (David E. Harper).

Atop the open cupola door are a handle and a sprung periscope cover. The stop-lugs on the left side of the cupola door hinge limited the rearward travel of the door when opened. Torsion bars inside the horizontal tube between the hinges assisted in lifting the heavy cupola door.

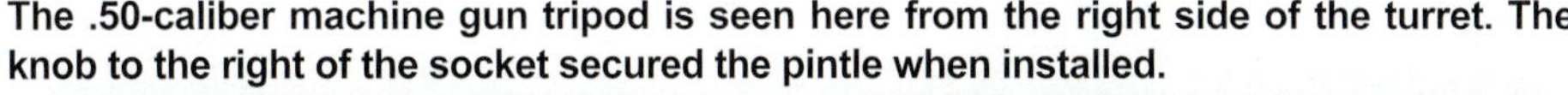

As viewed from behind the turret, the travel lock of the .50-caliber machine gun tripod is hanging loose, with the latch lying on the roof. A cap with a retaining chain is fitted over the pintle socket of the tripod.

The .50-caliber machine gun tripod is seen here from the right side of the turret. The knob to the right of the socket secured the pintle when installed.

This side view shows the holder, sprung latch, and the loader's door handle, intended to keep the open door from bouncing. One of the two inner handles/latches of this door is visible to the far right.

This overhead view shows the machine gun tripod between the open loader's hatch to the right, and the hinges of the turret storage box to the left.

As with most U.S. armored vehicles, the Chaffee was fitted with an M2 Browning heavy-barrel .50-caliber machine gun. The 61-inch long, 84-pound weapon has a maximum range of 4.5 miles, although the maximum effective range is a more modest 1.2 miles (David E. Harper)

The receiver of the .50-caliber machine gun was secured to the olive-drab cradle with pins, which in turn were secured with cotter pins. The large, round "disc" at the pivot point of the cradle is a spring equilibrator, which more or less kept the gun in a horizontal position.

The .50-caliber machine gun and ammunition tray and box are in place on this M24.

The antiaircraft machine gun was mounted on a tripod installed on the turret roof. A travel lock, shown here released, supported the weapon when not in use.

This wide-angle view into the open cupola of an M24 reveals the breech and recoil guard of the 75mm gun, as well as the commander's and gunner's seats. A reenactor is in the loader's position.

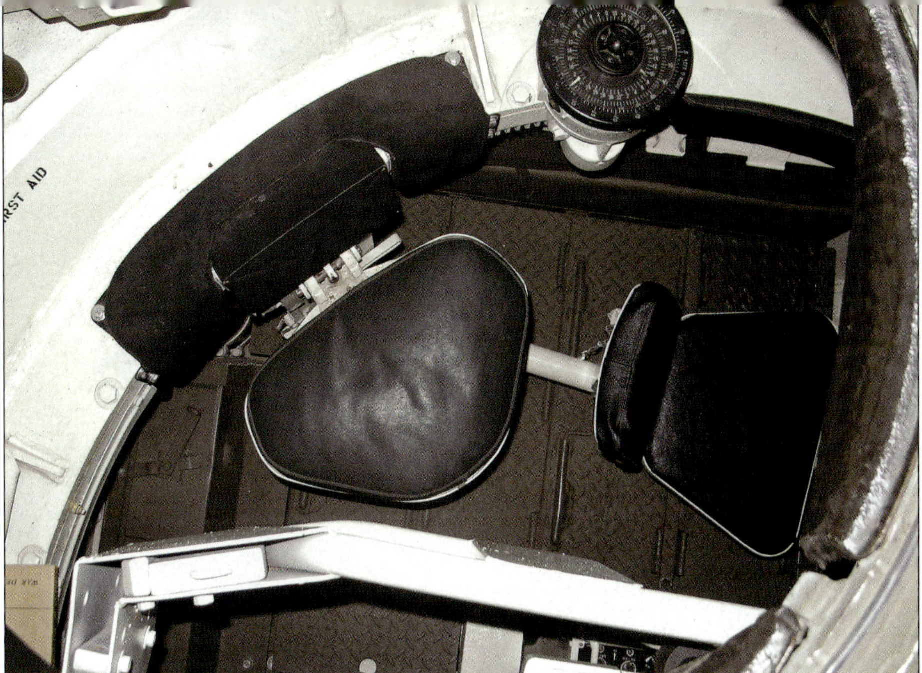

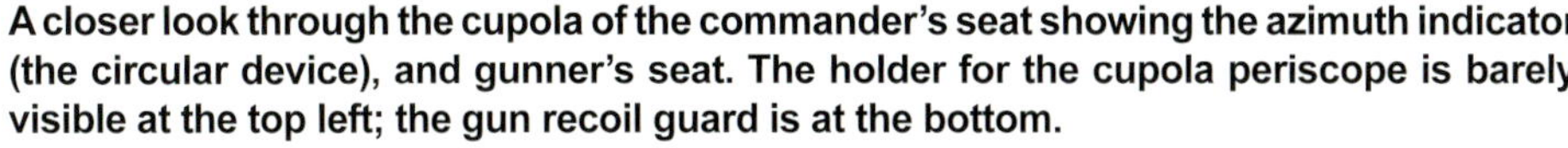

A closer look through the cupola of the commander's seat showing the azimuth indicator (the circular device), and gunner's seat. The holder for the cupola periscope is barely visible at the top left; the gun recoil guard is at the bottom.

Toward the rear of the turret is the radio. Strapped to the radio set is a rolled up canvas cover. At the bottom of the photo, a bracket holds the interphone control boxes for the loader (left) and commander (right). (Chris Hughes)

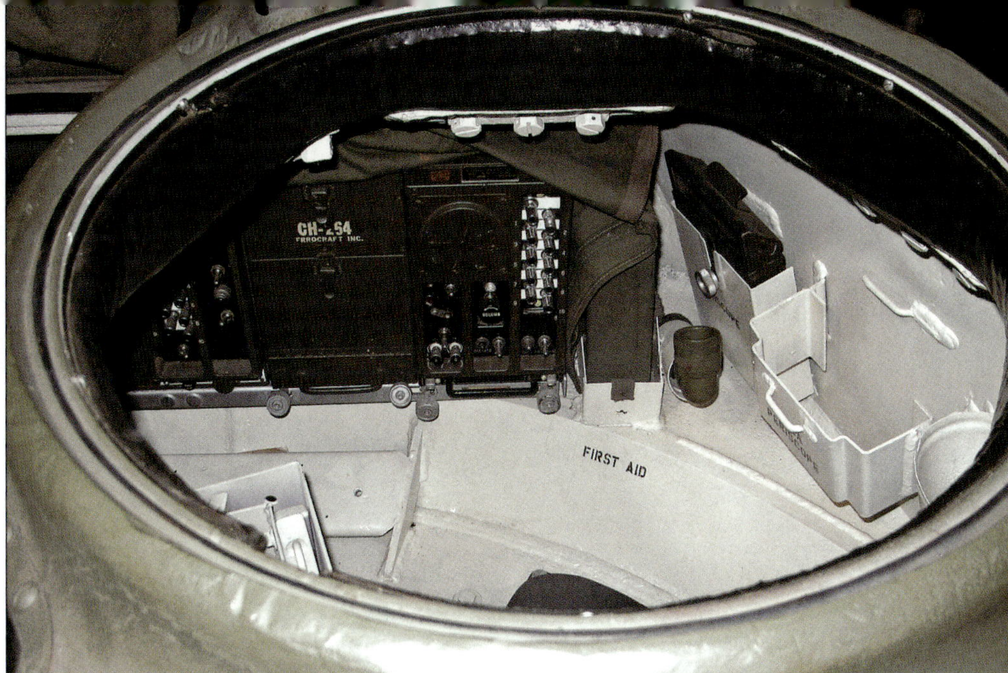

The canvas cover for the radio has been pulled back, revealing the transmitter (left) and receiver (right) inside the turret bustle. A periscope in its storage holder is to the right of the receiver, with the empty holder for the cupola periscope next to it. (Veterans Memorial Museum, Huntsville, Alabama)

A BC604 transmitter (left) and B603 receiver (right) comprised the SCR 508 radio package in the M24. Sometimes two receivers were installed. (Chris Hughes)

The port for ejecting spent 75mm casings is at the center of the photo; the operating arm/handle is fastened to a large lug projecting from the upper left corner of the door. At the bottom center is the loader's seat. (Chris Hughes)

Visible below the loader's seat is the turret ring gear. Like all the seats in the tank, padding was minimal and the form basic. For men who literally lived in the tank for weeks on end, the seats were adequate, but far from comfortable.

Turret Seat Assembly

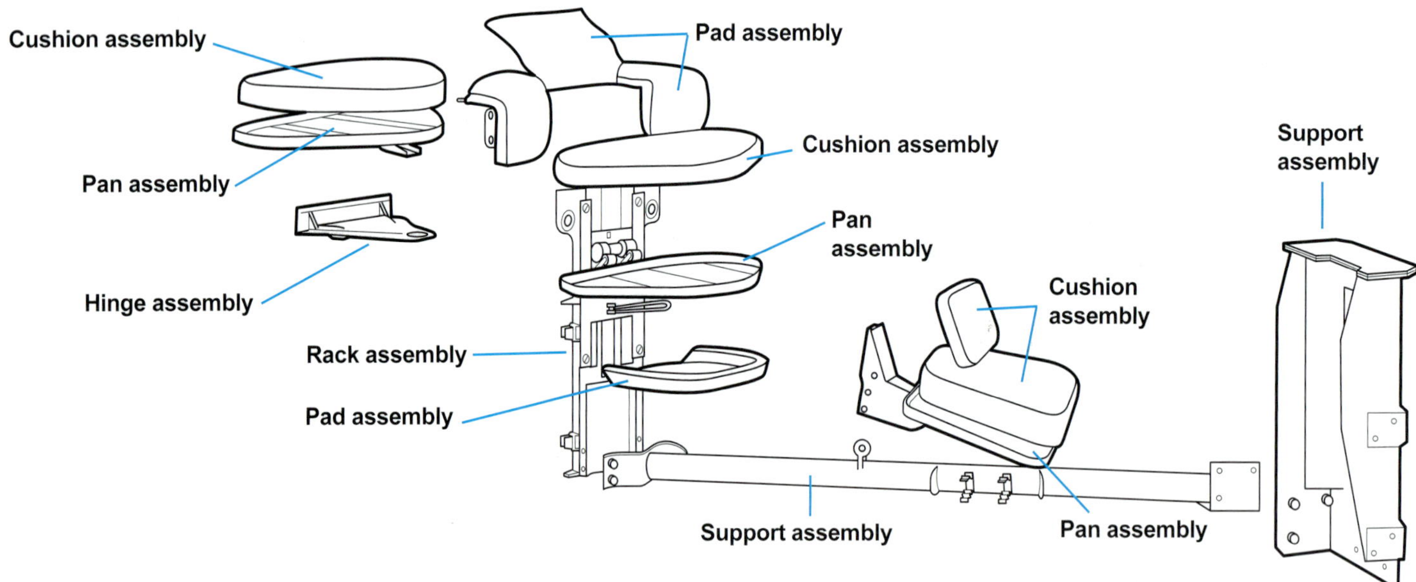

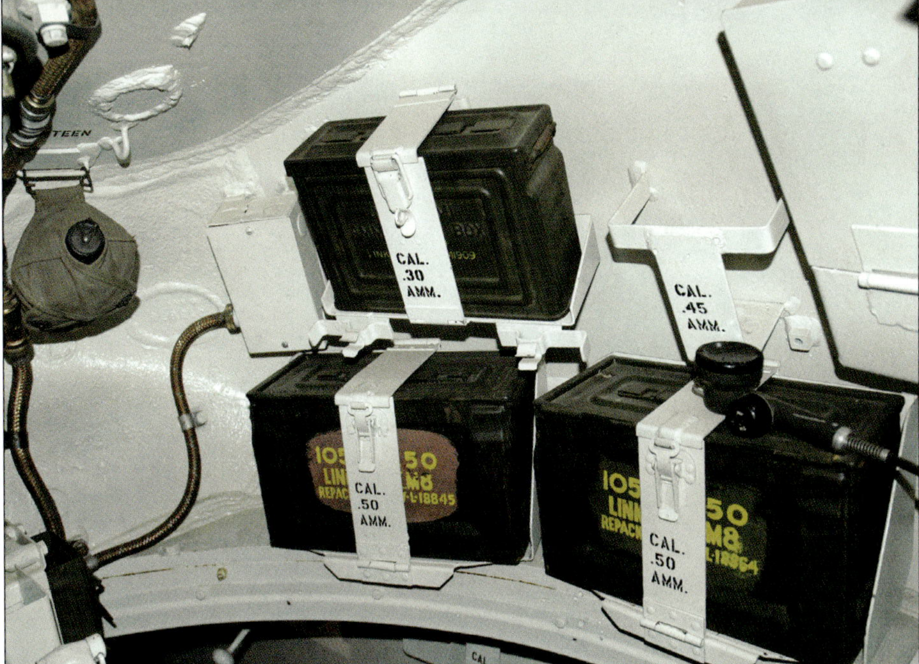

On the front right wall of the turret interior are storage racks for .30, .45, and .50-caliber ammunition boxes. At the front corner of the roof is the plugged opening for the smoke/ flare mortar that was used in early-production M24s.

Looking toward the front right of the turret, the mount for the coaxial machine gun (not installed) is to the left of center, with the .30-caliber ammunition box just visible below it. The black box above the coax mount is the oil reservoir for the main-gun stabilizer. To the lower left of the photo is the firing solenoid for the main gun, with related electrical conduits

Turret Weapon Positions

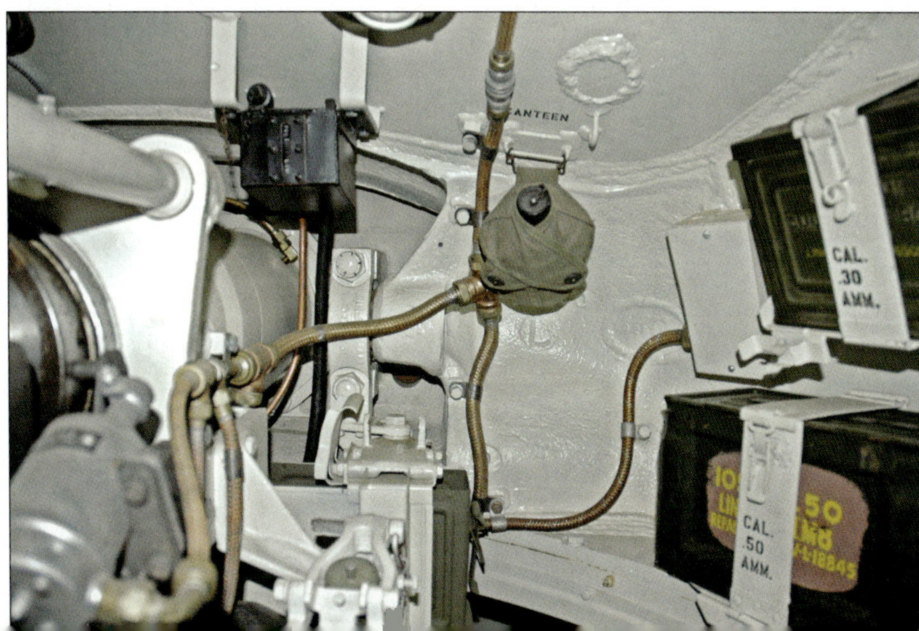

Smoke Mortar M3 installed in turrret

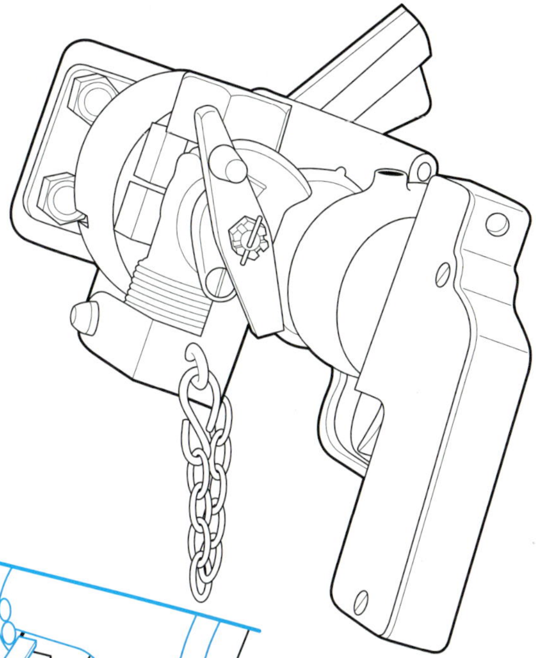

Guns installed in turret

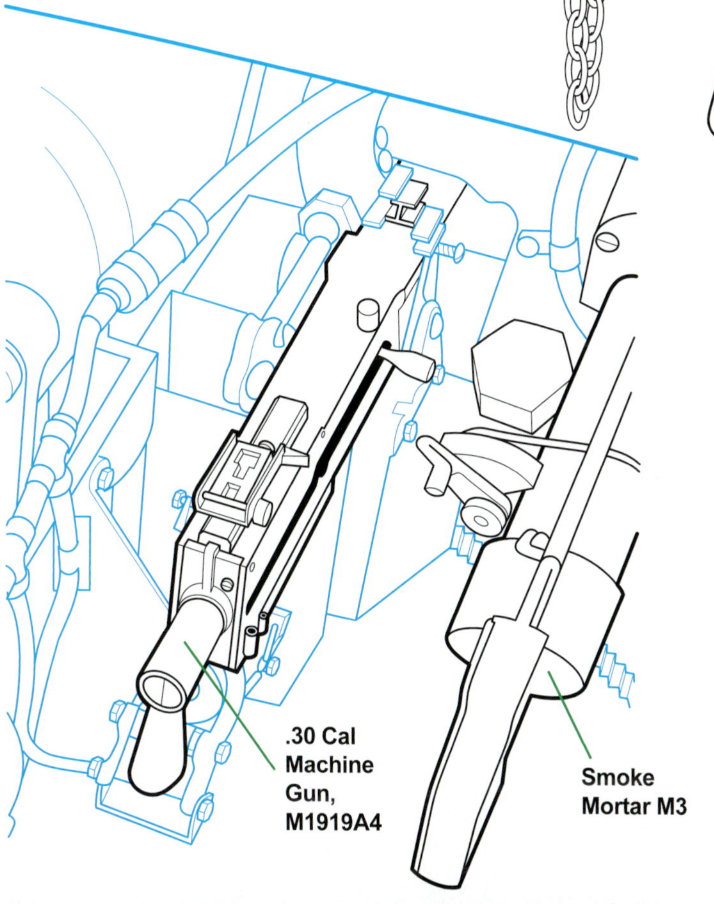

Visible in this view downward into the turret from the loader's hatch are, bottom to top, loader's seat, recoil guard, intercom control box, and commander's seat.

A very greasy breech area dominates the view toward the front of the turret. A breech operating lever would normally be mounted on the vertical, black column to the left of the breech. The manual turret traverse handle can be seen at the upper left of the photo.

The recoil guard, breech block, breech, and firing solenoid are seen in this view of the right side of the 75mm main-gun mount.

To the right of the main gun breech and breech block, the aluminum-colored firing solenoid can be seen. The round device at the center of the breech block is the firing lock; the two plugs on the left side of the rear face of the breech allow access to the shell extractor springs and plungers.

The tight quarters in the M24 turret are apparent in this view, facing to the front over the 75mm gun's breech. At top, two dome lights flank the roof bracket for the internal travel lock for the main gun. There is a related locking link atop the gun's recoil cylinder.

The 75mm breech, recoil guard, loader's seat, and turret floor, are seen here from overhead, through the loader's hatch. This well-worn vehicle exhibits heavy paint chipping and lubricant splatters on various parts.

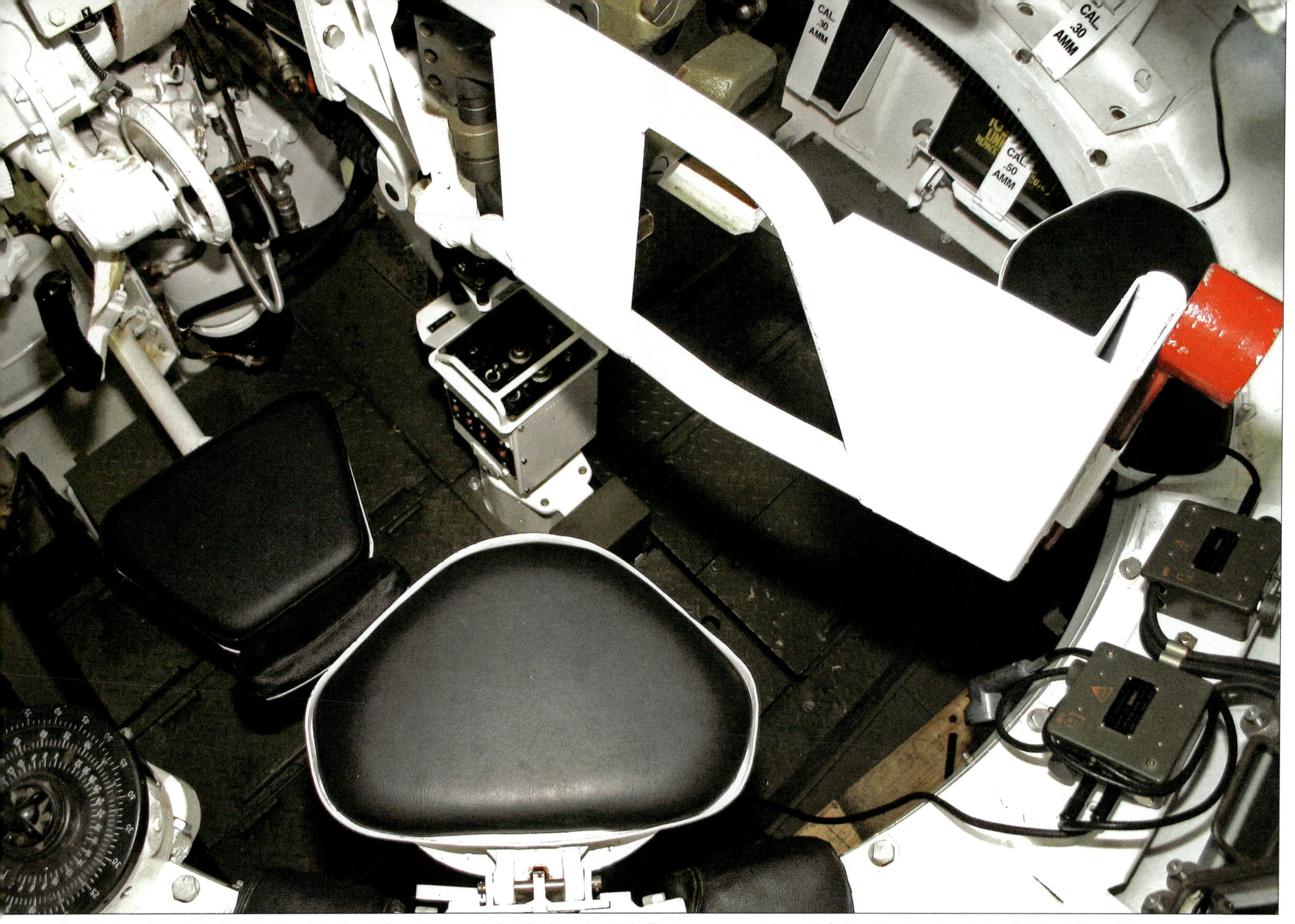

In this view down into the interior of the turret from the cupola hatch, the azimuth indicator appears at lower left, the elevating hand wheel at top left, and the commander's seat at lower center. The white device mounted to the floor below the recoil guard is the turret electrical control box, on which are switches that control such things as the turret traversing motor, gun stabilizer, and gun master switch. (David E. Harper)

A heavy wire guard on the top of the turret electrical control box helped prevent inadvertent actuation of the controls. The black panel on the side of the box consists of circuit breakers. (Veterans Memorial Museum, Huntsville, Alabama)

Projecting through the left side of the recoil guard is the breech-operating mechanism. When the gun was in operation, a breech-operating lever was mounted on the square lug just visible at the top of the mechanism, above the top rail of the recoil guard.

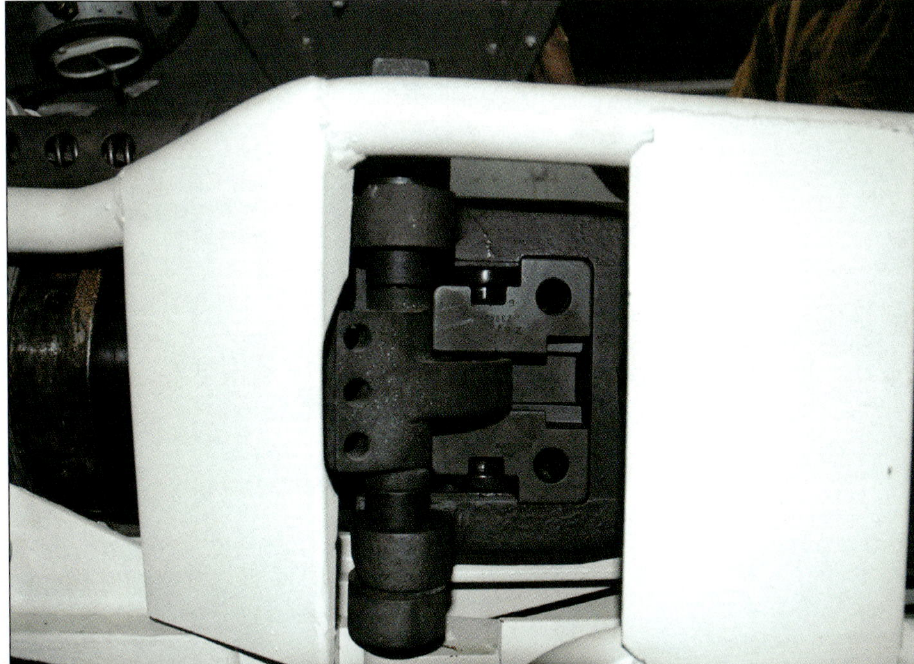

The 75mm gun's breech and recoil guard are seen here from the left.

Breech Assembly

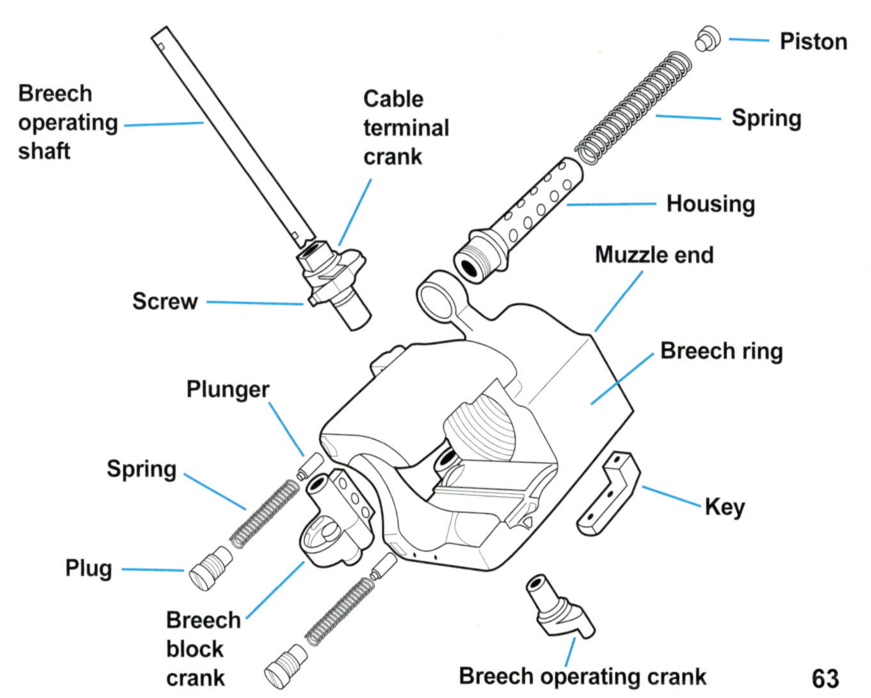

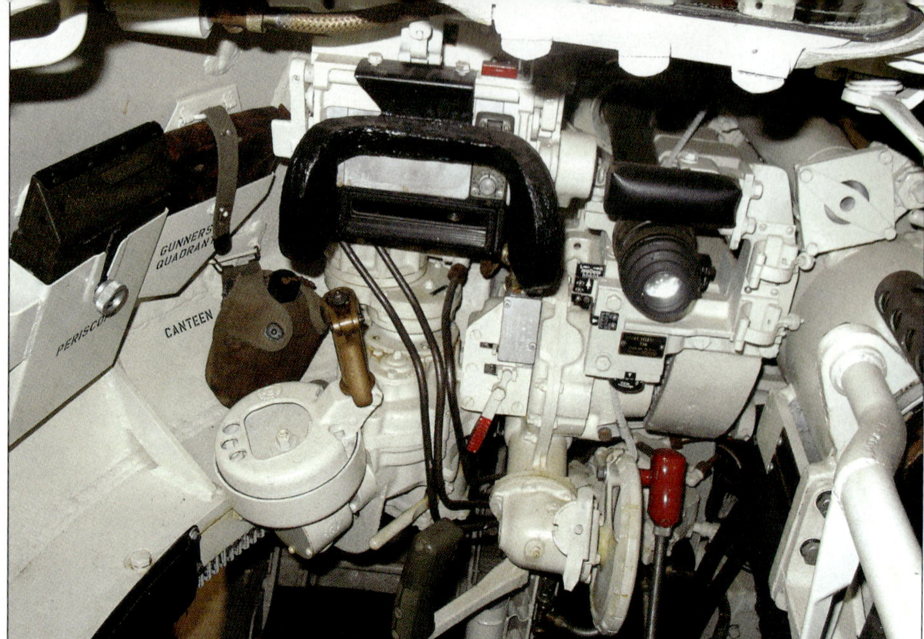

Most of the gunner's controls can be seen this photo. The periscope is flanked on the right by the telescopic sight. Along the wall to the left are storage brackets for a periscope, gunner's quadrant (for indirect-fire situations), and canteen. The lower part of a cupola vision block is at the top of the photo. (Veterans Memorial Museum, Huntsville, Alabama)

The mounts for the gunner's periscope and telescope are both fitted with padded headrests. A link to the front of the periscope allowed it to move in elevation with the gun. The periscope afforded the gunner a broad view of the target area, while the telescope had a smaller field of view but greater magnification than the periscope, allowing precision aiming of the gun.

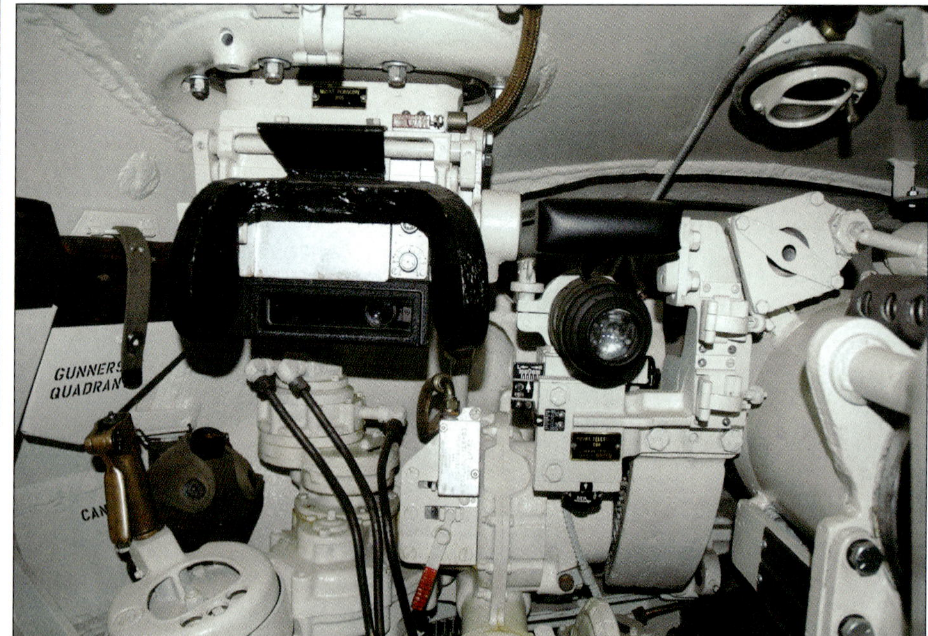

The gunner's seat is on a tubular mount. The controls to the front of the seat include the manual traverse wheel, hydraulic-powered traverse control (olive-drab pistol-grip handle), and elevating hand wheel. The gunner's telescopic sight is mounted coaxially with the 75mm gun. (Veterans Memorial Museum, Huntsville, Alabama)

The elevation linkage to the right front of the gunner's periscope (far right of the photo) allowed the periscope to elevate or depress in unison with the gun.

Vision-block retainer wedges, each secured to the cupola with three large screws, are visible in this view from below looking up toward the top of the cupola. There are padded head rests above the vision blocks.

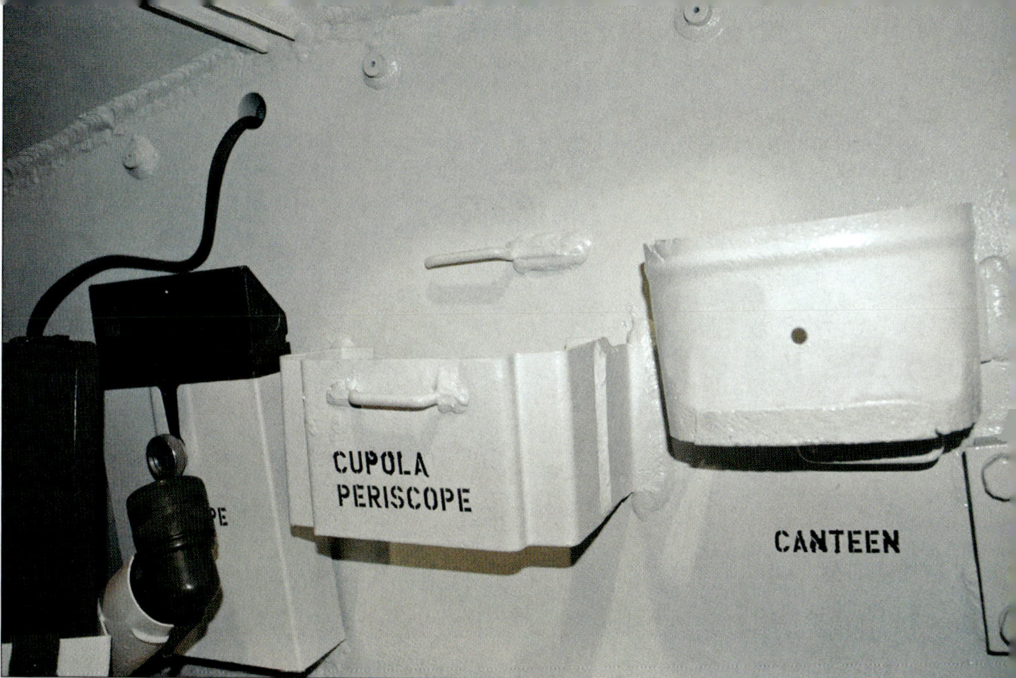

The storage array on the interior of the left side of the turret, next to the commander's and gunner's positions, includes, left to right: flashlight, periscope, binocular periscope for the cupola, and holder for binoculars, with a bar on the bottom of it for holding a canteen.

On the left side of the turret interior, next to the binoculars holder, is a box for hand grenades, underneath which is the azimuth indicator.

In the forward part of the turret ceiling are two dome lights, associated electrical conduits, an internal travel lock, and, toward the upper right of the photo, an opening for the turret ventilator blower (not installed). The cylinder at the bottom of the photo is the housing for the breechblock-closing spring.

Looking up at the turret ceiling from the commander's seat, with the front of the turret toward the bottom, the commander's turret traverse control is mounted to the transverse frame. This control allowed the commander to slue the turret while looking out through the cupola vision blocks or with his head outside of the cupola.

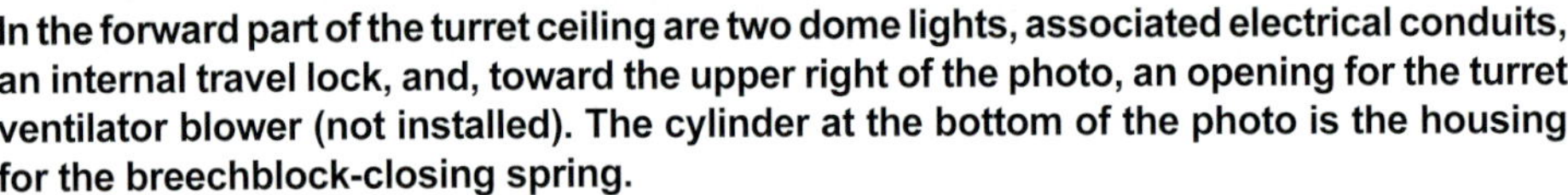

The turret control box is seen here from the gunner's position. The box was mounted on the floor of the hull, atop a collector ring (the olive-drab pedestal under the control). The mounting enabled the control to rotate in unison with the turret: a necessary measure, since the M24 lacked a turret basket.

The rear side of the turret control box is in the foreground, with the rear of the assistant driver's seat visible to the upper right of the photo. On the face of the control box are two large knobs controlling rheostats. The toggle at lower left is the gun master switch and above it the stabilizer switch. At right is the turret traversing switch.

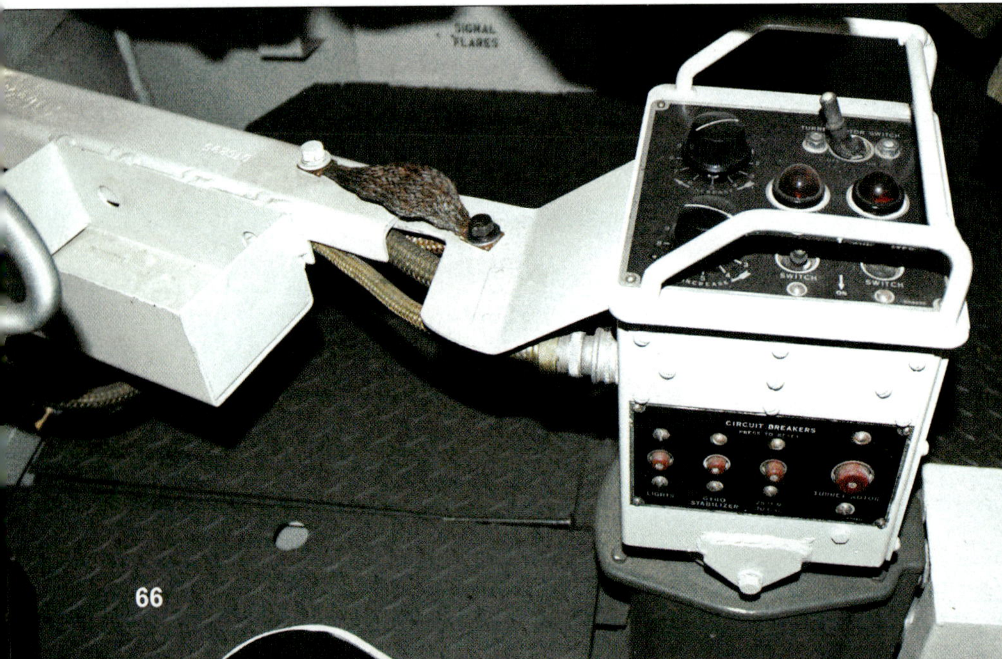

The power-traverse control handle (far left) and elevation hand-wheel (upper center) are seen here from the gunner's point of view. The black tube to the upper right is the stabilizer cylinder, which, as controlled by the stabilizer system, operated on the gun mount to keep its elevation on target as the tank moved.

Visible on the bulkhead in the left rear corner of the crew compartment, behind the commander's seat at center, are, left to right, the left generator regulator and starter relay and, just visible behind the commander's seat bracket, the left air cleaner.

The brass data plates can be seen in this gunner's view of the left side of the 75mm gun's cradle/recoil cylinder (white object to the center). Normal recoil was 11.5 inches. The button at the bottom center is the manual firing plunger.

At the center on the bulkhead to the rear of the turret, as seen from below the turret, is the right air cleaner and duct. The large box below the duct is the right generator regulator, below which is the right starter relay. To the right of the photo is a ventilating door which, when opened, allowed the engine fans to draw foul or smoky air out of the crew compartment.

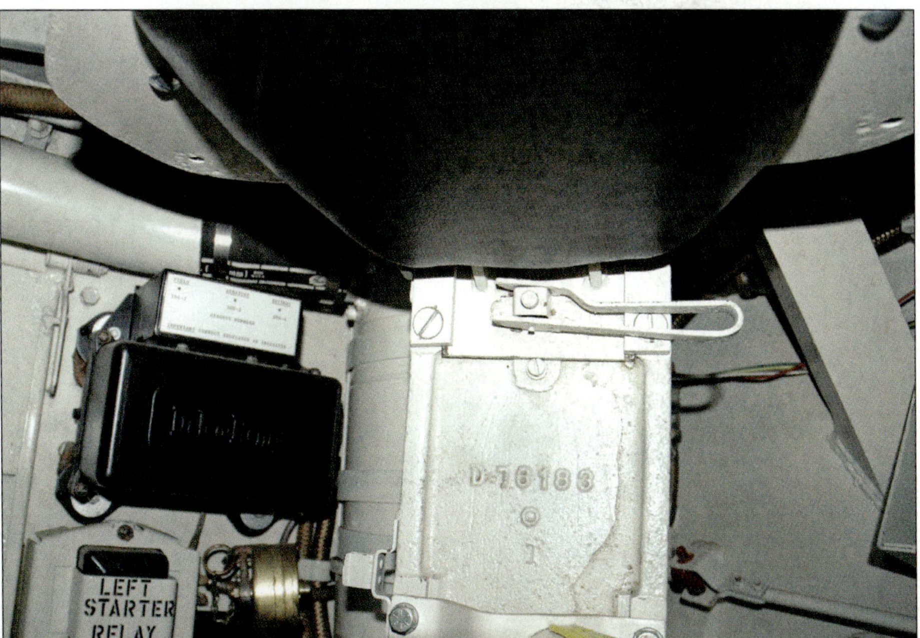

The red cylinder projecting from the hull floor toward the bottom left is the fixed fire extinguisher. The manner of attachment of the gunner's seat rail to the bottom of the commander's seat bracket is apparent. Also visible are the turret ring gear and storage brackets for .30-caliber machine gun ammunition boxes on the side of the hull.

Storage brackets for ammunition boxes, an oil can, and intercom phone line the left side of the hull. There is a brace welded to the hull plate toward the left of the photo.

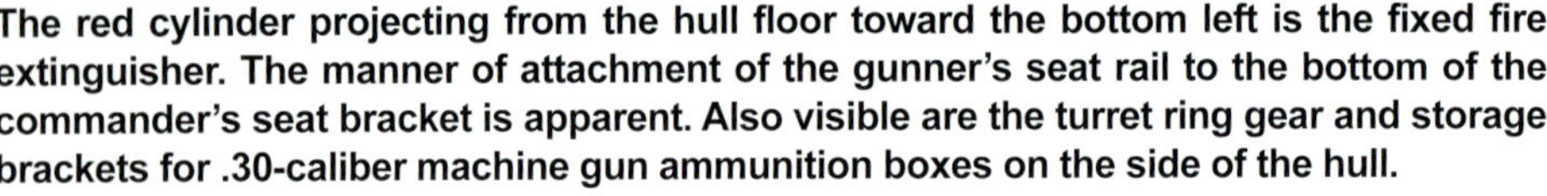

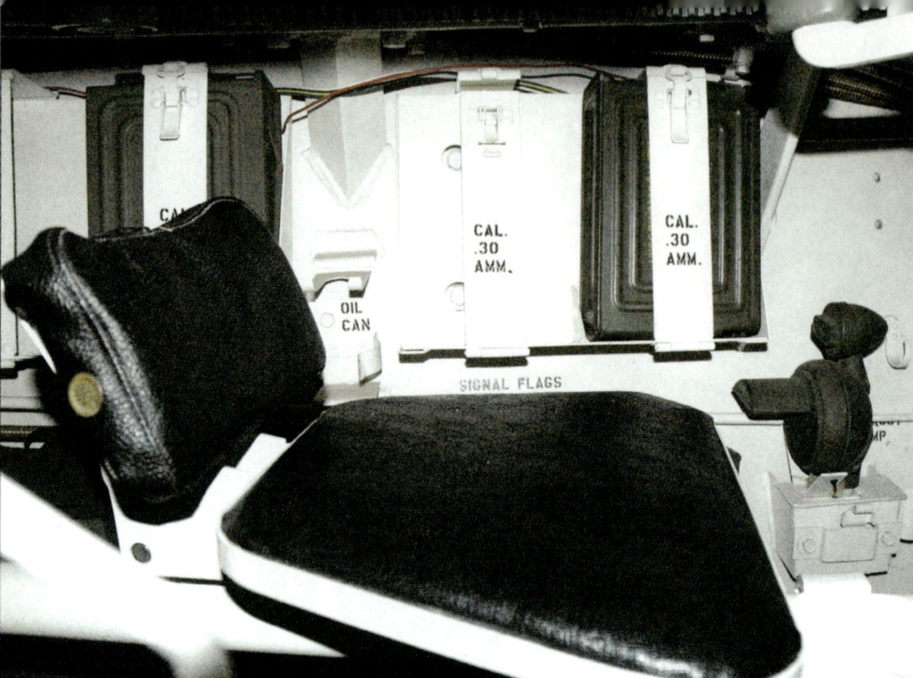

On the inside of the hull beside the gunner's seat (on the back rest of which there is a breather vent) are storage brackets for ammunition boxes, oil cans, signal flags, and spare headlight units.

A reenactor settles down into the driver's seat in this view of the left side of the hull interior. Directly behind him on the ceiling is the operating lever for his door, or hatch. To his side, on the wall, is a bracket for an M3 .45-caliber "Grease Gun" submachine gun.

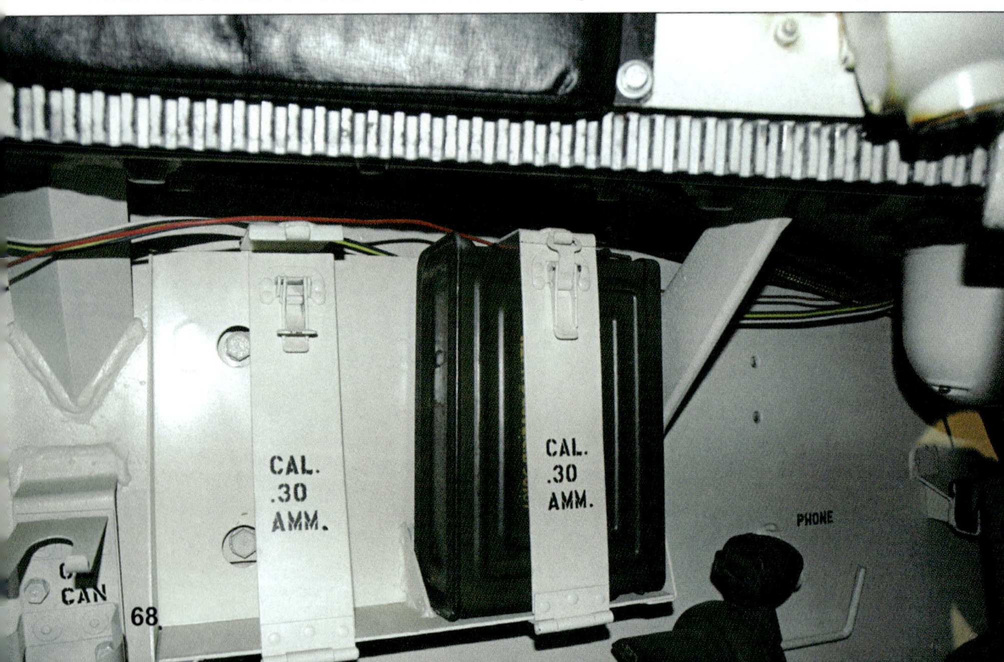

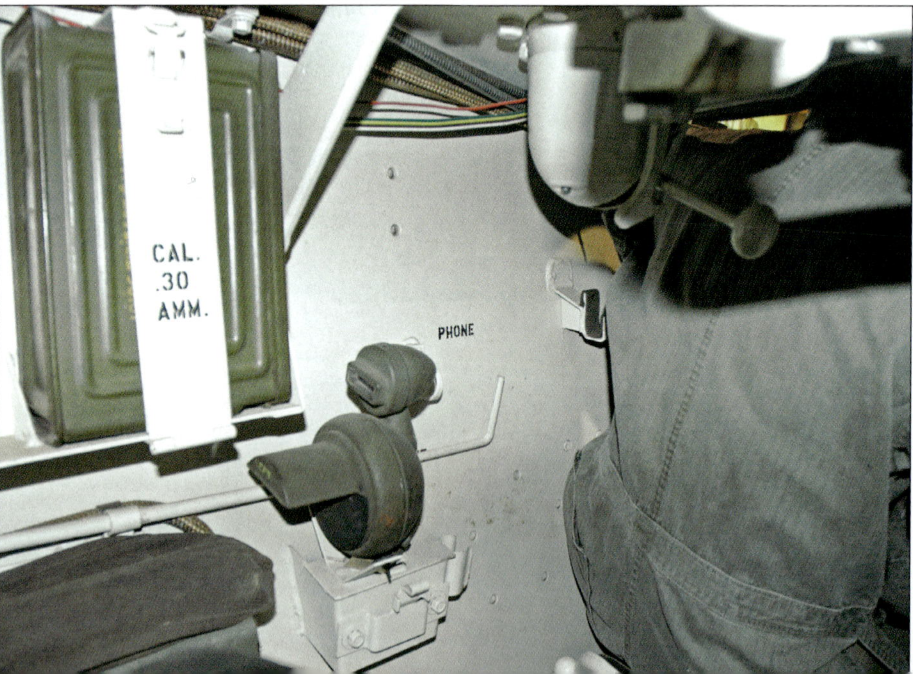

The driver's seat is seen from overhead through the driver's hatch. A support assembly, seen in front of the seat, facilitates seat elevation, so the driver can operate the tank with his head outside the hatch. (Veterans Memorial Museum, Huntsville, Alabama)

A view through the driver's hatch toward the tank wall reveals data plates, storage brackets for an M3 submachine gun, a map clip, and, to the side of the seat, the left steering lever. The "box" with a filler cap on top to the rear of the driver's seat is an oil can that was a standard component. (David E. Harper)

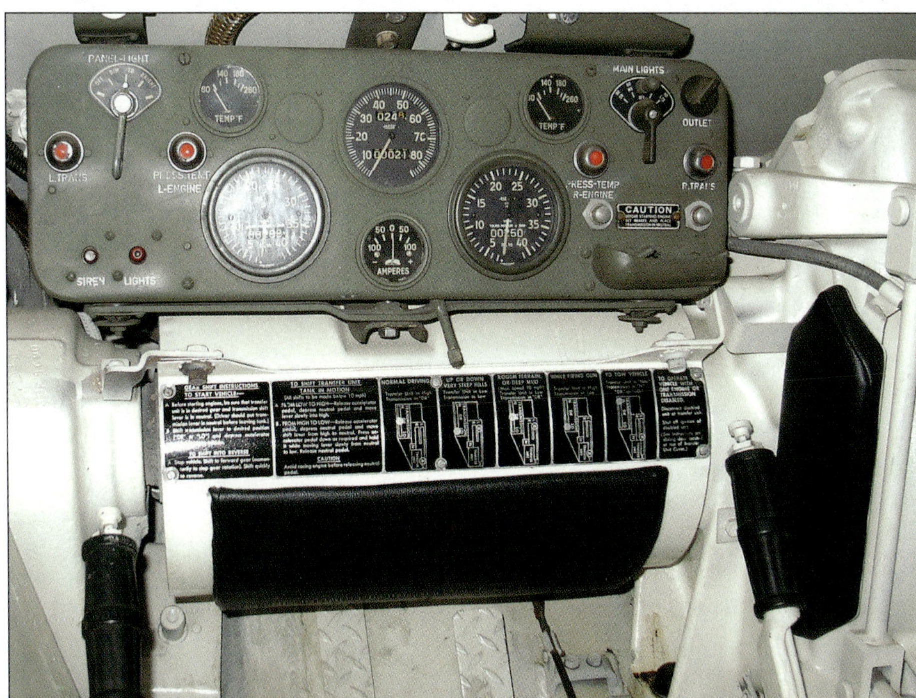

The driver's instrument panel is mounted to the front plate of the hull. Data plates on the final-drive propeller shaft cover explain how to operate the transmission selector lever and transfer unit lever. Below the plates is a protective pad for the driver's knees; a smaller knee pad is on the side of the controlled differential case. The handles of the steering levers are at the bottom. (Veterans Memorial Museum, Huntsville, Alabama)

The driver's foot pedals between the two steering levers are, left to right, the siren button (to right of left steering lever grip), transfer-case neutral pedal, and accelerator pedal. Braking of the M24 was effected by pulling back on both steering levers simultaneously. (Veterans Memorial Museum, Huntsville, Alabama)

On the left side of the driver's position inside the M24 there are stowage brackets for one of the M3 "Grease gun" submachine guns provided for the crew. (David E. Harper)

The components of the instrument panel are, top row, left to right: panel lights switch, temperature gauge, speedometer, engine temperature lights, main lighting switch, electrical outlet; center row: red warning lights; bottom row: circuit breakers, left engine tachometer, ammeter, right engine tachometer, and starter switches over ignition switches. A manual, self-locking throttle is mounted on the white bracket over the center of the instrument panel.

A driver's-eye view across the controlled differential toward the assistant driver's station. The receiver of the glacis-mounted .30-caliber machine gun and the spent-casing collector bag are visible. The red cap at the center of the photo is for the differential oil filler tube.

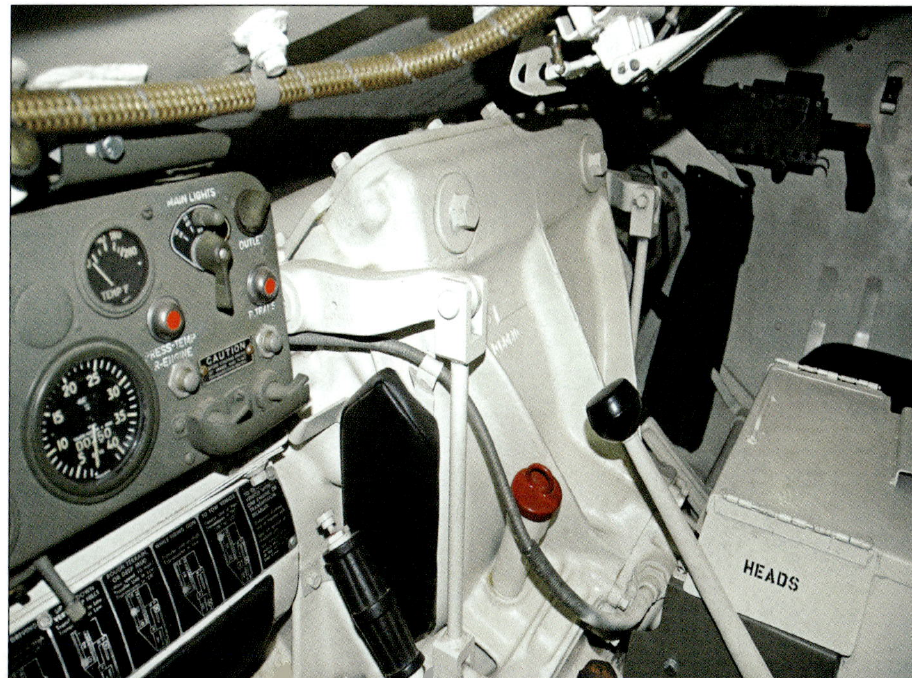

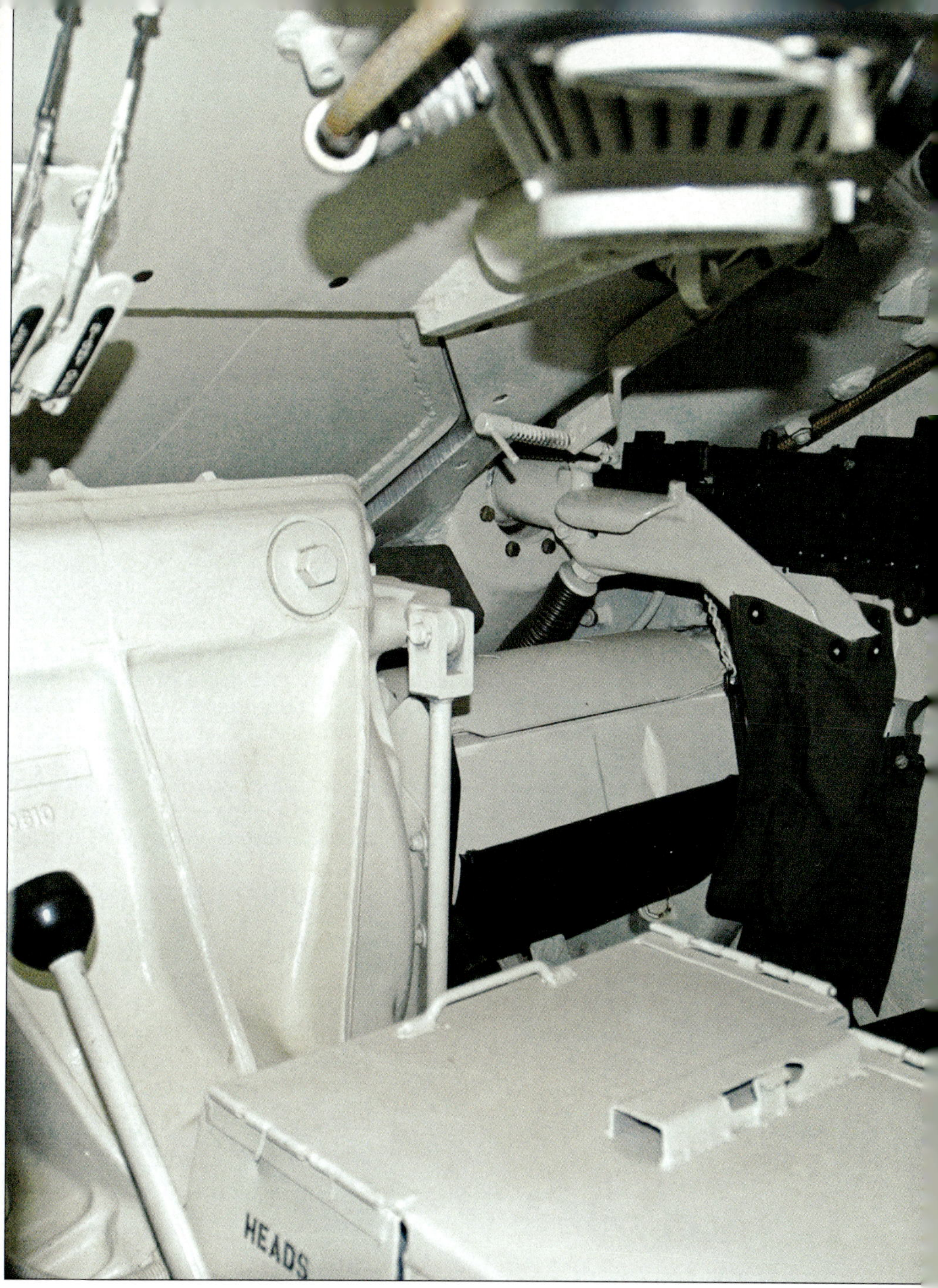

As viewed from the driver's station, the bottom of the ceiling ventilator is at the top center of the picture. To its right are the locking handles for the assistant driver's door. The fuel pump controls are at the upper left of the photo.

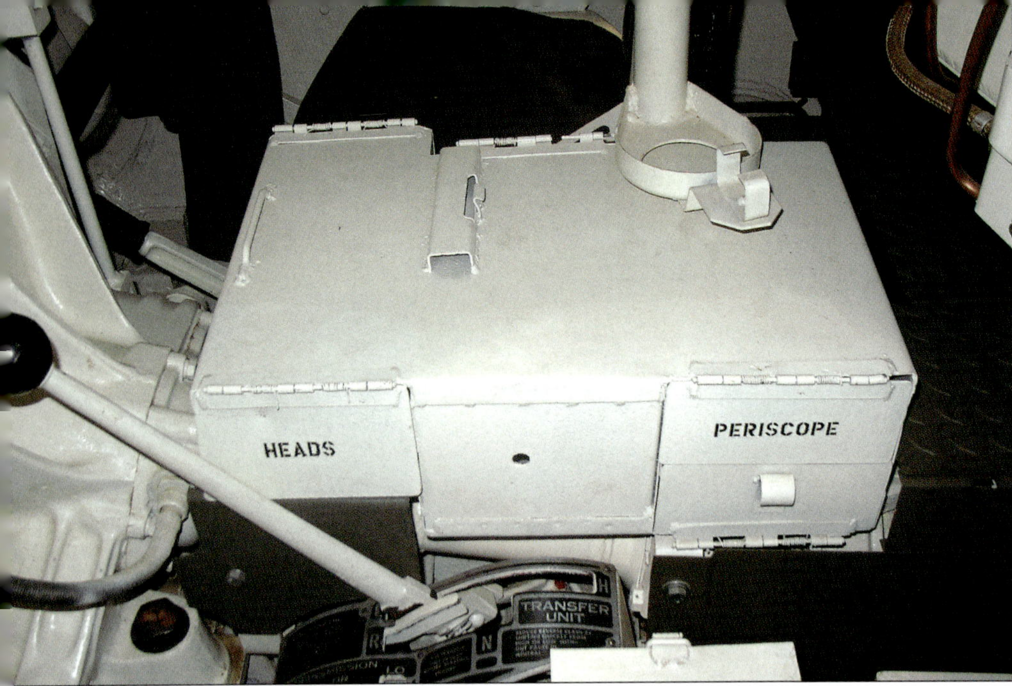

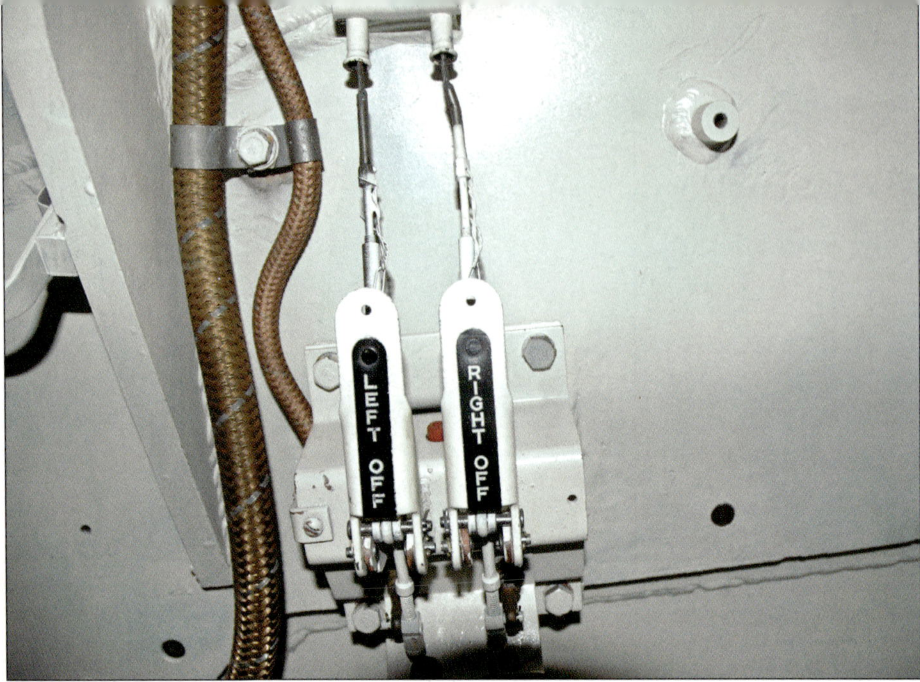

In this view from the driver's station, the shifting lever for the transfer unit is in the foreground. Above it is a storage box for a periscope and spare periscope heads, beyond which is the assistant driver's seat. To the left of the photo is the rear part of the controlled differential. (Veterans Memorial Museum, Huntsville, Alabama)

The ceiling and open hatch appear to the upper right in this view from the assistant driver's position toward the top of the front hull plate. To the right of the frame member are a dome light, travel lock for the glacis machine gun (in its stowed position), and the open assistant driver's hatch.

Mounted at the center of the front plate of the engine compartment, the fuel pump levers control the fuel shut-off valve and the power feed to the left and right fuel tanks. Pulling a lever up closes the valve and shuts off the fuel pump to the related tank.

This other view from the assistant driver's position shows the edge of the controlled differential at lower left, along with the dome light, travel lock, and glacis machine gun. The coil spring on the travel lock kept the unit tight against the front plate of the hull when not in use. The front cover plate, which allowed access to the controlled differential, is at the lower left.

The view through the assistant driver's hatch shows his dual steering controls. A map clip is on the side wall and a lever for raising the seat can be seen to the right front of the seat cushion.

The .30-caliber glacis machine gun is visible in this view through the assistant driver's hatch toward the front of the tank. Running laterally across the photograph is the final-drive propeller shaft cover. Like the driver, the assistant driver had protective knee pads on that cover and on the side of the controlled differential.

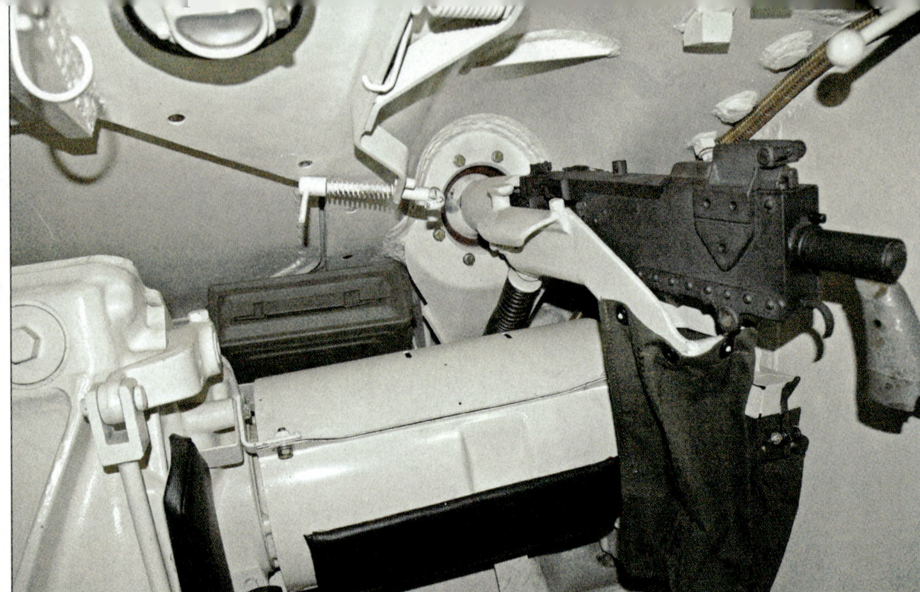

The equilibrator spring on the underside of the machine gun cradle, the spent-casing collector bag, and the .30-caliber ammunition box in front of the cover on the final-drive propeller shaft are visible in this view from the vantage point of the assistant driver in the M24.

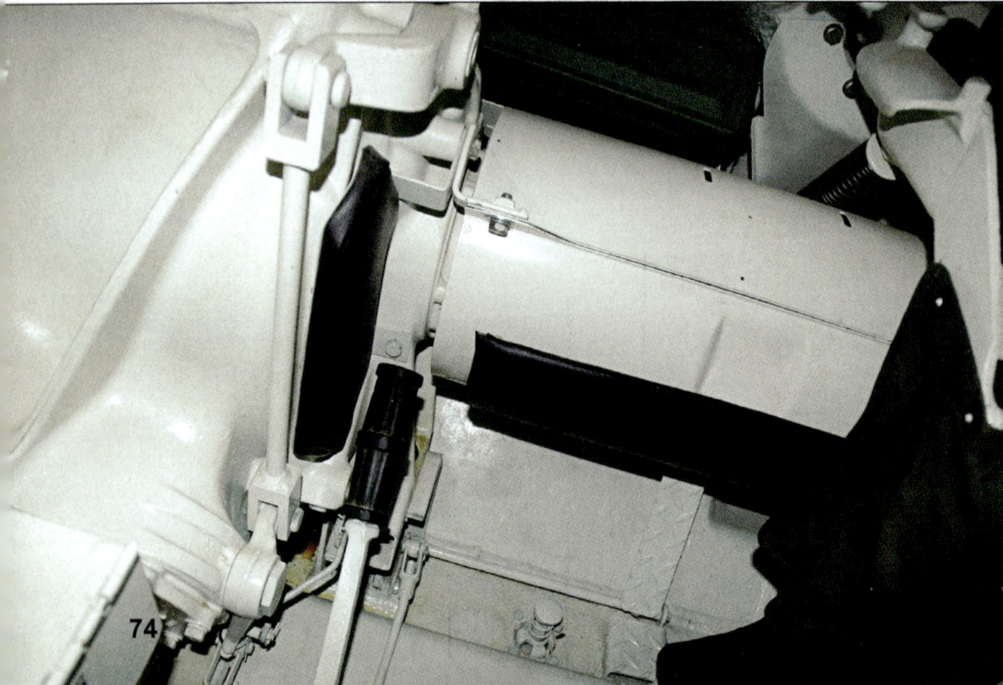

The large, vertical shaft, seen here from the assistant driver's position, is the right-hand link for the steering brake in the controlled differential. The smaller-gauge link immediately to the right of the steering lever is for the accelerator pedal; when the assistant driver was not controlling the tank, he was to disconnect this link.

In this photo, the .30-caliber glacis machine gun has been removed from its cradle to reveal the collector bags for spent casings (left) and links (right). To the right is one of two storage brackets for an M3 .45-caliber submachine gun. (Veterans Memorial Museum, Huntsville, Alabma)

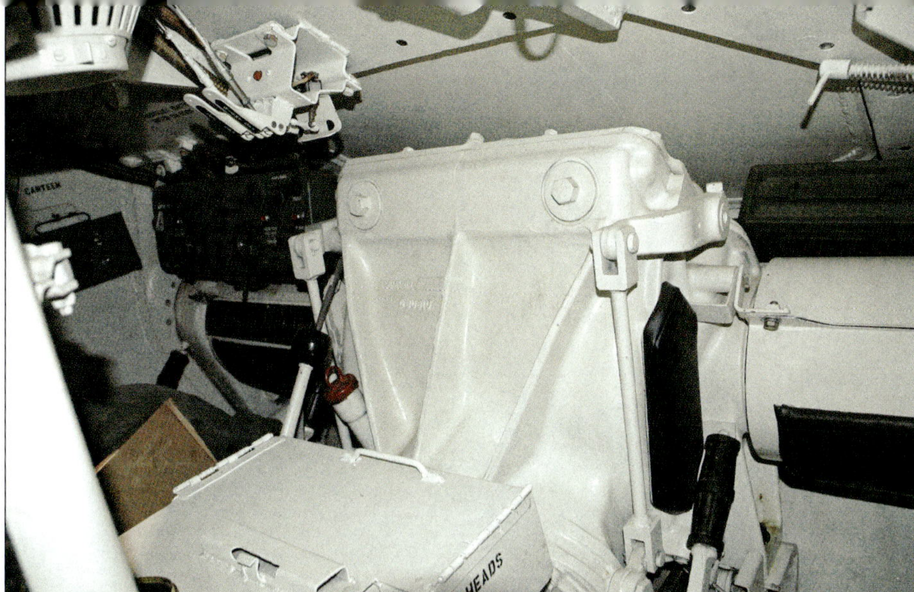

The ventilator and the fuel pump controls can be seen toward the upper left in this view of the driver's compartment from the assistant driver's seat. The large hex bolts at the top corners of the controlled differential are for adjusting the steering brake bands.

The doors of the periscope and periscope heads storage box are sprung so that they remain in a closed position.

Hanging from a hook between the fire extinguisher at left and the interior light at right is a handheld microphone for use with the vehicle's intercom. (David E. Harper)

In this view of the driver's station from the assistant driver's seat, the controlled differential is to the right, the periscope and periscope head storage box are in the center, and floor plates are to the left. Control links and hydraulic lines run under the periscope box.

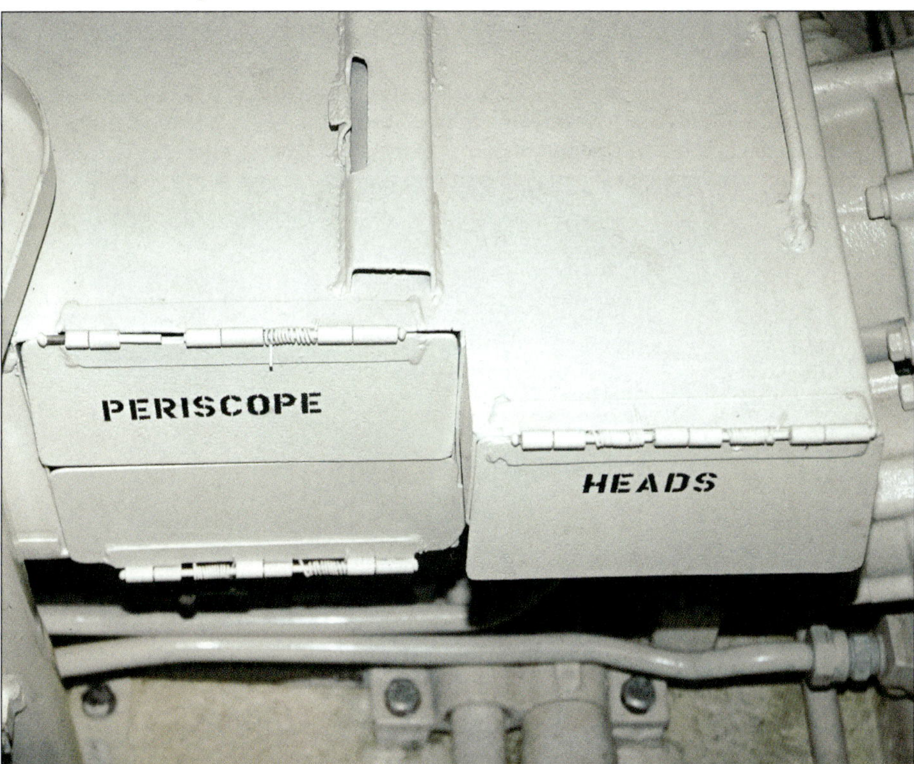

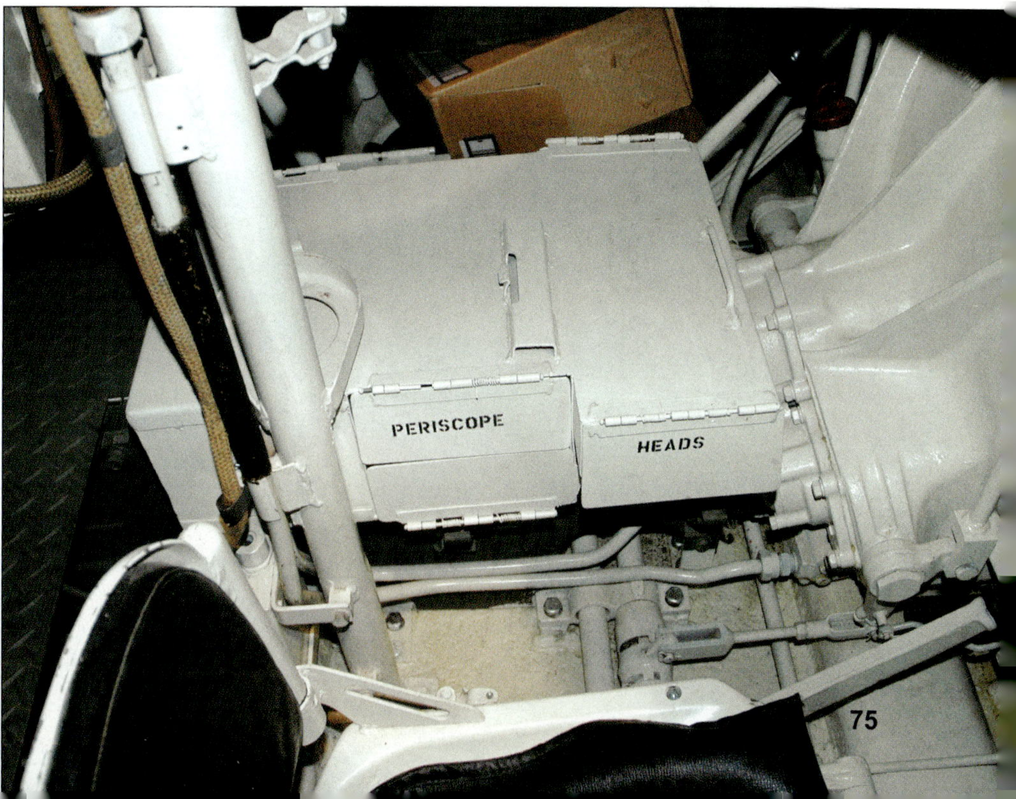

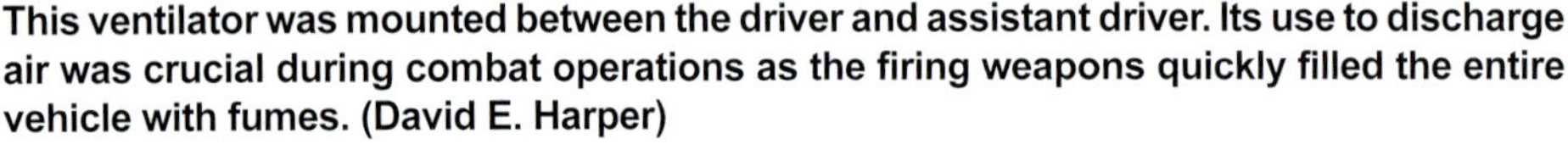

This ventilator was mounted between the driver and assistant driver. Its use to discharge air was crucial during combat operations as the firing weapons quickly filled the entire vehicle with fumes. (David E. Harper)

The turret control box (center) appears here as seen from the assistant driver's station. To the right is the white guard for conduits leading to the gyro-stabilizer and traverse motor. To the rear are the driver's and commander's seats. The ventilator door on the rear bulkhead is to the left of the turret control box. (Veterans Memorial Museum, Huntsville, Alabama)

The ventilator blower in the ceiling of the drivers' compartment (seen here from the assistant driver's seat) has two-way switching to draw fresh air into the tank or blow out foul air. The control switch is on the rear of the blower, out of view. A dome light is next to the blower, and the fuel pump controls are to the far right. Notice the turret ring gear to the lower left.

As seen from the assistant driver's seat, the turret traverse motor is left of center, to the rear of the ventilator blower. The traverse motor was hydraulically powered, but it could be disconnected and the turret traversed manually using a hand wheel.

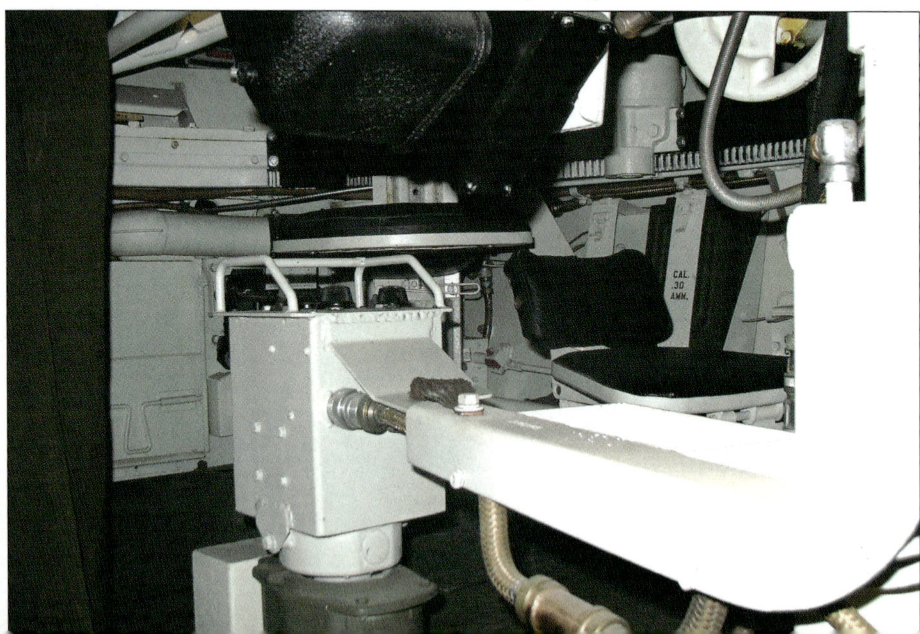

Reduced, Normal, and Supercharge HE Rounds

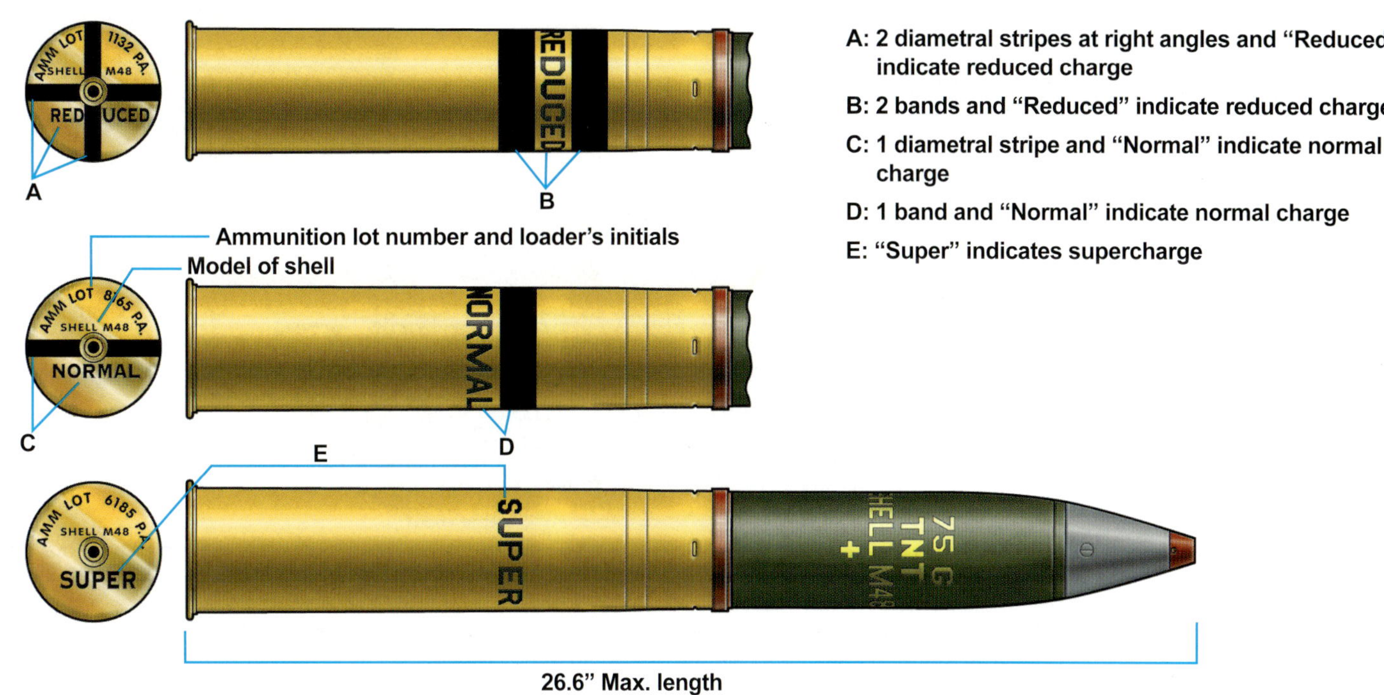

A: 2 diametral stripes at right angles and "Reduced" indicate reduced charge

B: 2 bands and "Reduced" indicate reduced charge

C: 1 diametral stripe and "Normal" indicate normal charge

D: 1 band and "Normal" indicate normal charge

E: "Super" indicates supercharge

Shell, Fixed, Smoke, WP, M64, W/Fuze, PD, M48A3, for 75-mm Guns

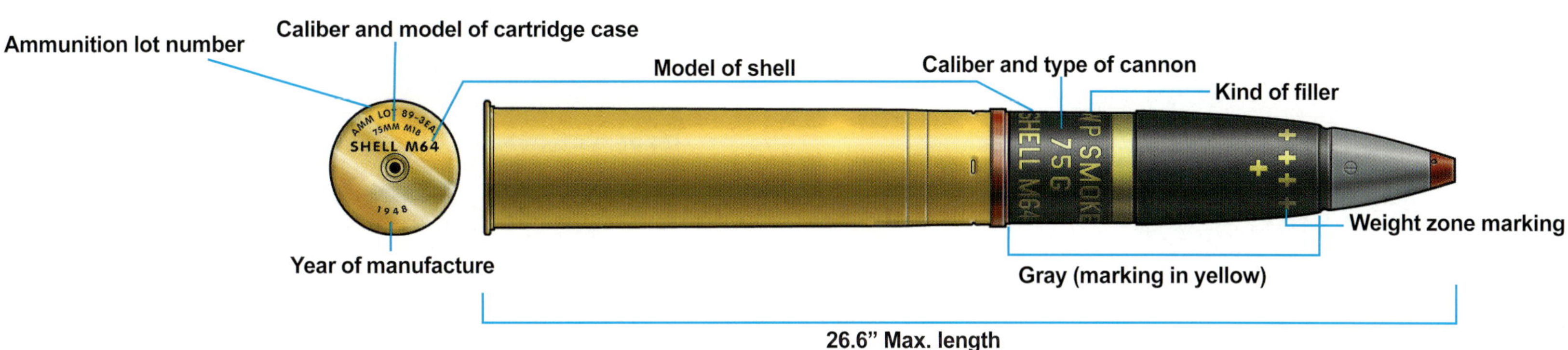

The "Ally Oop III" operated in northwestern Europe in January 1945. A roll of camouflage netting was strapped to the rear fender of the Chaffee.

An M24 of the 81st Reconnaissance Squadron, 1st Armored Division, served near Bologna, Italy, towards the end of World War II.

The "Rebel's Roost" with the Tank Platoon of the 24th Reconnaissance Company, 24th Infantry Division, the first U.S. tank to engage the enemy in Korea, completed combat near Chonui, South Korea, in July 1950, where troops could relax and attend to domestic-type chores.

An M24 of the 45th Infantry Division, 245th Tank Battalion, deployed on the dusty roads of South Korea in the summer of 1950 with this equipment.

An M24 appeared in this configuration at the 80th Ordnance Base Depot, Tan Son Nhut, South Vietnam, in 1967.

"Cleo," registration number 30139138, conducted maneuvers in Alaska in 1954, sporting a broom and carrying 5-gallon cans on the front of the hull.

An ARVN M24 parked at Tan Son Nhut in South Vietnam wore a paint scheme of brown and dark green sprayed over Olive Drab.

An M24 of the 18th Cavalry Reconnaissance Squadron, 14th Cavalry Group, deployed whitewashed to camouflage it for European winter conditions in Petit-Thier, Belgium, in early 1945. Sand shields have been removed from the fenders, exposing mounting brakets.

An M24 of the 43rd Cavalry Reconnaissance Squadron, 26th Division, appeared in this configuration near Saarburg, Germany, on 13 March 1945.

The M24 "Hannibal" carried a .50-caliber machine gun at a target range. The machine gun included a flash suppressor on the muzzle.

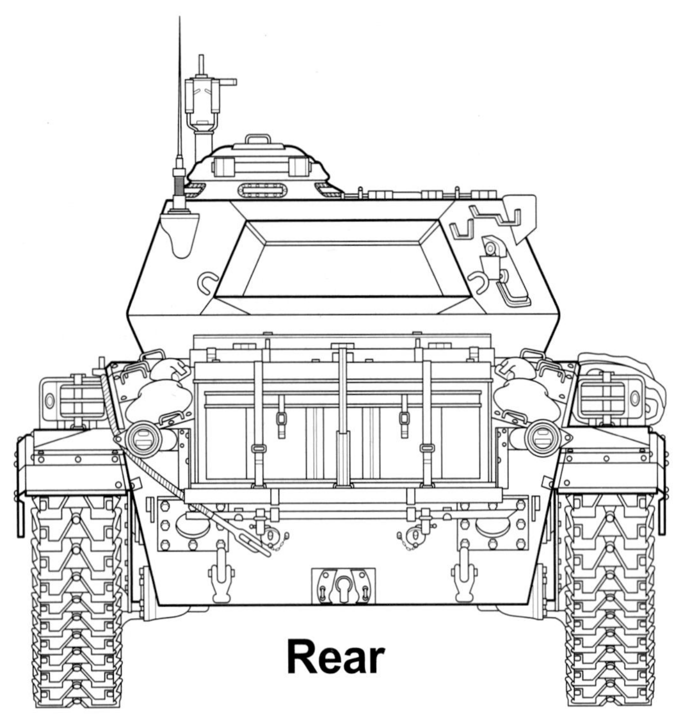

Rear

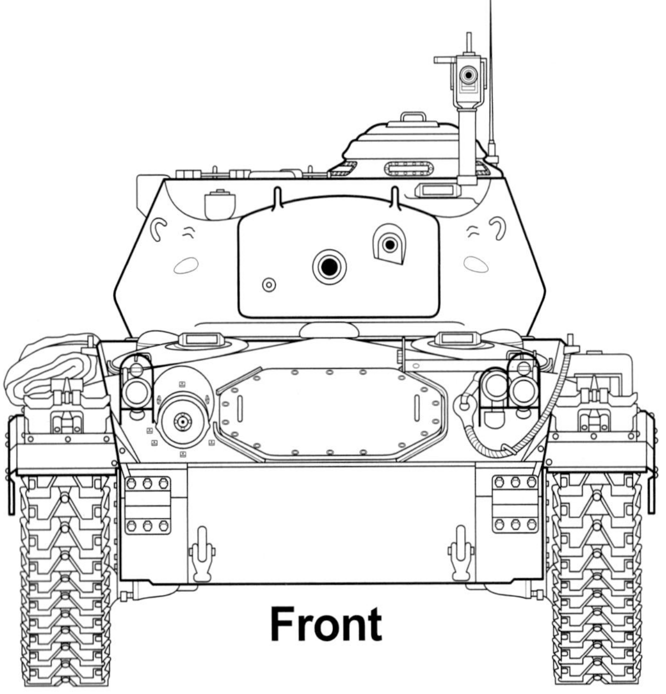

Front

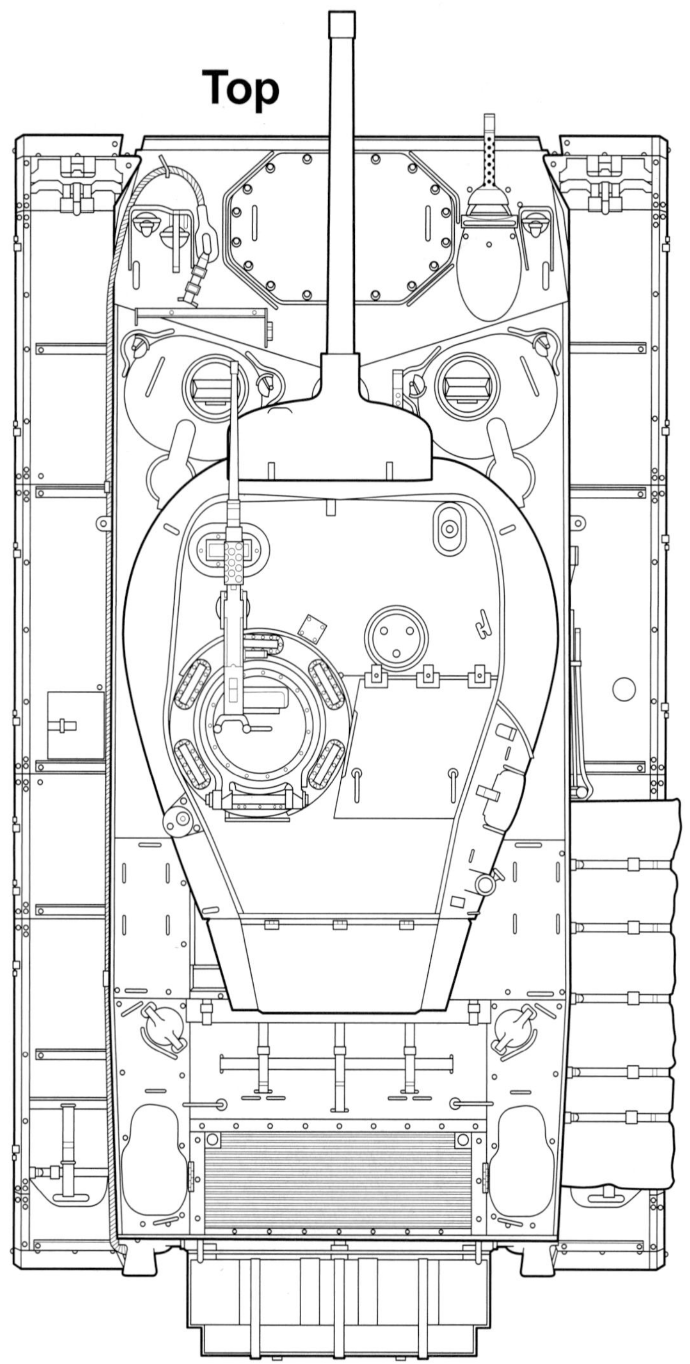

Top

General Data

Model........................M24
Weight....................40,500 lbs
Length.....................216 inches
Width......................117 inches
Height.....................97.5 inches
Tread......................96 inches
Track Width...............16 inches
Crew.......................4 or 5
Maximum Speed.......34 mph
Fuel Capacity............110 gallons
Range......................100 Miles
Turning Radius.........23 feet
Armament Main.........75mm
Secondary.................2 x .30
Flexible......................1 x .50
Electrical........24-volt negative ground
Hydramatic Trans-
mission Speeds..........4
Transfer Speeds........2

Engine Data

Engine.....................2 x Cadillac 44T24
Number of Cylinders......90 degree V-8
Cubic Inch
Displacement..................................349
Horsepower...............110@ 3,400 RPM
Torque......................240 @ 1,200 RPM
Governed Speed.............Not governed

Radio Equipment

The Chaffee was fitted with the SCR
508, 528, or 538 radio set in its turret.
Command tanks also had an SCR 506
in the hull.